GB: MASTER, MONSTER or MYTH?

GB: MASTER, MONSTER or MYTH?

A biography of

Geoffrey Bolton (1893–1964)

Nicholas Aldridge

ARTHUR H. STOCKWELL LTD
Torrs Park   Ilfracombe   Devon
Established 1898
www.ahstockwell.co.uk

British Library Cataloguing-in-Publication Data.
A catalogue record for this book is available
from the British Library.

ISBN 978-0-7223-3904-6
Printed in Great Britain by
Arthur H. Stockwell Ltd
Torrs Park   Ilfracombe
Devon

DEDICATION

To Christopher (*Christophoro*
In Latin, *meo Domino*)
My patron since those days of yore
(In fact since 1954),
When we were young and fit and free
In daily contact with GB.
We often trembled at his bellow,
Enjoyed his company when mellow
His mood became if Sussex won:
He could be fierce, he could be fun,
Sometimes a monster, sometimes kind.
Will anybody ever find
What was the truth and what the myth?
My modest effort comes herewith;
And with nostalgic backward look
To you I dedicate this book.

Christopher and I were contemporaries at Summer Fields, Eton and Cambridge. During our last year at Summer Fields (1953–4), I lived mainly in the eighteenth century and, having decided that I would be a poet, naturally I thought that I ought to have a patron. And there, in our midst, was my friend Christopher Bailey, heir to a barony. Better still, he had a beautiful sister, Susan, for me to be hopelessly in love with, of course. Ah me! Happy distant days!

CONTENTS

Glossary: Initials and Nicknames 9

Preface 11

Introduction 13

Chapter 1: Boyhood and Education 21

Chapter 2: War 37

Chapter 3: Summer Fields 53

Chapter 4: Life and Literature 67

Chapter 5: Fifth Form 77

Chapter 6: Partnership 93

Chapter 7: War Again 107

Chapter 8: Mid-Century Blues 119

Chapter 9: Headmaster 131

Chapter 10: Retirement 141

Chapter 11: The Immortal Part 149

Bibliography 153

Index 154

GLOSSARY: INITIALS AND NICKNAMES

Aunt Margaret: Margaret Alington, née Maclaren, wife of EHA
BA: Bachelor of Arts
Bam: G. W. Evans
Bear: Revd E. H. Alington
Bloody Bill: H. K. Marsden
Bobs: A. F. Alington, youngest son of EHA
Bogi: Fifth Form B
Bollosh/Boltosh: Geoffrey Bolton
Budge: E. J. H. Dixon
Common E: The Common Entrance exam
CO: Commanding Officer
Crab: J. F. Crofts
Doctor: Revd C. E. Williams
Dogbags: Dr Williams
DSO: Distinguished Service Order
EFB: Eric Bowtell
EHA: Revd E. H. Alington
G&S: Gilbert and Sullivan
GB: Geoffrey Bolton
Gill: Gillian Alington, née Tanner, wife of A. F. Alington
Gluggins: Gloucestershire
Golgotha: Geoffrey Bolton
HKM: H. K. Marsden
HM: Headmaster
HMM: Hubert Mullins
HWLH: Harold Hartley
JFE: John Evans
JLB: Jimmy Bell
JPM: Pat Marston
Liz: Revd J. A. C. Lysaght
MA: Master of Arts
MC: Military Cross
MCC: Marylebone Cricket Club
MP: Member of Parliament
Mrs: Gertrude Maclaren, née Talboys, wife of Archie Maclaren
OS: Old Summerfieldian (plural OSS)
OUCC: Oxford University Cricket Club
Patters: lawn tennis
Perdie: Perdita Marston, née Williams, wife of JPM
Ping-Pong: F. P. Penny
PGW: P. G. Wodehouse
PMBS: Patrick Savage
Polyglotshire: Northamptonshire
Puss: Nicholas Henderson
Ranji: K. S. Ranjitsinhji

SF: Summer Fields
Shark(y): John Evans
Smee: Patrick Macnee
Stodge/Stodgy: A. W. H. Thompson
Tab: Cantabrigiensis, i.e. a member of Cambridge University
Tark(y)/Ticky: John Evans
Teddies: St Edward's School
The Buzzer: The school shop
The Little Man: Mark Faber
Uncle Hugh: Revd E. H. Alington
VPSC: Varsities and Public Schools Camps
Wuggins: Worcestershire

PREFACE

'THIS IS A BOOK that should have been written long ago.' So begins GB's *History of the O.U.C.C.*, and, though *he* may merely have been displaying his usual modesty on that occasion, the same is undoubtedly true of this attempt at a biography of him. The feeling grew upon me that *somebody* ought to try to put GB down on paper before all memories faded, and gradually it began to look as though it would be me. 'Oh well,' I thought, 'I might do it one day,' and I drew up no plan of campaign. When Summer Fields celebrated its 125th anniversary in 1989, among the many who came to join in the festivities was GB's younger sister Angela, very cheerful and full of life and memories. I determined to visit her and have a good long chat about Sussex childhood, etc. But I was dilatory, and in 1993 the annual magazine which we sent her was returned with the sad word 'Deceased' stamped on the envelope. I had left it too late.

This book is also a fraud because, although I purport to be the author, large chunks of it are not written by me. I toyed at one stage with simply annotating GB's own *Recollections of Summer Fields*. Two factors decided me against that course. It would have become an unwieldy mass of footnotes, giving it a spurious and offputting appearance of scholarliness. Secondly, GB says, and said, virtually nothing about his schooldays, the Great War and his part in it, the Sussex Martlets, his younger colleagues or individual boys. If this now appears a mere 'paste with trimmings' job, I am sorry; but at least I enjoyed doing the job. It has been a labour of love, and it could not have happened without help from a large number of people, many of whom, sadly but not surprisingly, have not lived to see its publication. These must all now be regretfully prefixed with 'the late':

Eric Bowtell, Harold Clayton, Tim Cosford, Harold Fawcus, Mike Gover, Eddie Harrison, Roger Jacques, Perdita Marston, Patrick Savage, Henry Shaw, E. W. Swanton, Richard Usborne and Simon Wright.

Equally helpful, and as far as I know still with us, have been:

J. H. Akerman, Jonathan Alexander, Jonathan Balcon, Edward Blain, Robin Broke, Alex Churchill, Rory Darling, Robin Darwall-Smith, Hubert Doggart, Roderick Dunnett, Toby Eady, Richard Elliott, R. R. G. Gardner, Mr and Mrs M. J. Gould, Gavin Hannah, Joan Hartley, Charlie Hartridge, Derek Henderson,

Charles Hossell, Ralph Hulbert, Nigel Kitchen, Rob Lagden, Susan Martineau, Russell Muir, Penny Noble, Nigel Pearce, Dominic Price, Alison Rae, Alan Readman, Christopher Snell, Chris Sparrow, Brian Straton-Ferrier, Gay Sturt, Chris Swift, Ian Tamworth, Peter Ward and Judith Waters.

G B,
GEOFFREY BOLTON
30th July 1893 – 20th April 1964

INTRODUCTION

"THE ONLY MEMORY that I have of G. Bolton is that he was extremely fierce and all the boys were terrified of him. He looked like a skeleton as he was gassed in the First War." – *Summer Fields boy of the 1930s.*

"GB . . . certainly had defects of personality, but not, I submit, defects of character. It is to him that I owe my entry into the brilliant world of Homer (as well as the pecuniary attainment of an entrance scholarship); to him I owe much of my French – and the memory of digressions and conversations on many subjects, and the discovery of much English literature. Conservative and authoritarian to his fingertips, GB could still delight in, and communicate to us his delight in, Lytton Strachey, H. G. Wells and Bernard Shaw." – *Summer Fields boy of the 1920s.*

"How that gaunt figure dominated my five years! I loved and revered him, and was terribly afraid of him . . ." – *Summer Fields boy of the 1930s.*

"I suspect that I was a rather uninquiring boy who assumed that headmasters were likely to be pretty odd. Clearly GB was very odd to look at, but I suspect that in other ways he was dead straight and fairly un-noteworthy from a boy's perspective. We knew where we stood." – *Summer Fields boy of the late 1950s.*

* * * * *

"Cave, GB!"

The words still bring a frisson down the years. It is at once both easy and hard to evoke GB upon the printed page – easy because so many myths bring him to life, hard because it is impossible to summon up all one's senses at a time, smell the Turkish cigarette, wince beneath those bony fingers, gaze at the pale Oxford bags and faded blue-green tweed and hear those tones, a little husky when at peace, or fulminating in a fast and furious roar.

Physically, he was not unlike two mid-twentieth-century actors, Ernest Thesiger and Wilfred Hyde White, but without the finicky effeminacy of the former or the bumbling bonhomie of the latter. The words 'gaunt' and 'skeletal'

13

leap to the pen describing him. He was fantastically thin, from his narrow head and shoulders down to his bony ankles. The story is told (and this verse of the GB apocrypha I do believe to be true) that, when he had to have an injection, Sister Beadon asked him to take down his trousers and then burst out laughing: there was nothing to stick the needle into! If this recollection seems disrespectful, I hasten to say that it is not my intention to demean GB or even necessarily to demythologise him, though I shall attempt to focus his 'myth-master-monster' image if I can. His thinness may have been congenital but sharpened by his experiences in the Great War. It is becoming hard for us really to know what those who went through it suffered, despite the ever increasing amount of paper and film that is yearly expended on it, often with artistry and sincerity.

For forty-one years, GB was a schoolmaster at Summer Fields, Oxford, intensely dedicated to the life of the school but not without other interests. He rose through the ranks, from assistant master to become a partner in 1930, assistant (or possibly co-) headmaster in 1939, and finally headmaster in 1956 – too late fully to enjoy it, though he made some useful and overdue changes to the school. After four years he was forced to retire on doctor's orders. He was also the president of the Sussex Martlets for fourteen years and a devoted historian of Oxford University cricket. It is hard to tell how good (or bad) a cricketer he actually was. Several authorities describe him as an indifferent performer, and he was certainly nowhere near first-class or university standard. But he did bowl regularly for his various clubs, and took wickets. There is a scrap of old film, taken c.1944, which shows him bowling in the nets at Summer Fields. He has an idiosyncratic style – left-arm-round with virtually no use of the right arm at all – perhaps its eccentricity mesmerised batsmen.

The essential GB was a mystery and a myth: so much of what one remembers about him was fantastic, or verges on fantasy, that one is not quite sure whether it was true or *bien trouvé*, or if one had imagined it. Was he really gassed in the Great War; and was that what made his hair prematurely white? In fact, it was not so remarkably premature as folk memory suggests; if one looks at the school photographs, his hair was not really white until he had passed forty. In the 1919–22 photographs he has brown hair; in the late 1920s and early 1930s he becomes increasingly grey. On this subject, his only comment was a facetious riposte:

"Please, sir, why is your hair silver?"

"Can't afford gold, boy."

And what about the belief that he chewed every mouthful twenty-three times, or that he knew the whole of the *Iliad* and the *Odyssey* by heart, and would recite them when he could not get to sleep, taking them up at the line where he had left off last time? In many ways he was the typical schoolmaster (it was not done, or it was infra dig, to refer to 'teachers') of the first half of the twentieth century – with heavy Victorian overtones – after all, his most formative years had been in Victoria's reign, and her influence continued well beyond the Edwardian era. But in other ways he was exceptional: a phenomenon; a crank; a bigot; a single-minded, dedicated worker who never spared himself; a figure of terror; an inspiration – all these and more. One

One of the few good photographs of GB as a young man comes in this 1922 group; he is sitting between 'Bam' Evans and Bryan Buckley, and behind them stand L. A. G. Strong and 'Liz' Lysaght. The boys in this photograph, their names all filled in by Ian Tamworth, are (top row) R. M. Sandbach, N. de B. Priestley, David McKenna, H. L. S. Sikes, I. F. R. Cunynghame; (middle row) D. E. O'Rorke, E. B. Butler and (front row) R. M. Branwell. Priestley was one of the boys who gave GB strife when he started teaching – the 'tough eggs' mentioned on page 59. David McKenna was one of two brilliant all-round brothers; the year after this picture he tied with Bernard Burrows as the top Kings Scholar at Eton – a unique achievement. He was one of Summer Fields' original governors in 1956. Branwell was an outstanding cricketer and presented the batting cup which is still awarded annually.

cannot expect to unearth some easy answer as to what made him tick. He was a complex character, dominant yet shy, who was, like all those involved in war, the victim of circumstance, but who managed to rise above the horror and the reaction without cynicism and with gratitude. 'With my usual luck' is a phrase he uses more than once in his memoirs.

His great loves were Summer Fields, scores of individual boys, cricket, P. G. Wodehouse, Gilbert and Sullivan, Shakespeare and Homer, and classical and English literature in general. The linking of these loves – introducing boys to the classics, cricket, Gilbert and Sullivan and P. G. Wodehouse – was his life's work between 1919 and 1960.

The 1920s, the decade when he came into his own as a schoolmaster, was an age of amiable dottiness – relief from the war, perhaps – and of fantastic clothes: the blazer and the boater, Oxford bags, plus-fours, plus-eights and a wide assortment of strange costumes for men and women, including co-respondent shoes, gloves and hats. (Did GB ever wear a hat, other than a cap for cricket? Yes. I have recently come across a film showing him watching cricket in a blazer and boater: he looks ready to go on the musical-comedy stage.) People dressed and spoke like characters in a Wodehouse story – which is hardly surprising, as they were the models for them. Labels abounded. Boys were frequently told that they were 'blithering idiots' or had 'a yellow streak'; these epithets endured and might hurt, but it did not do, of course, to show vulnerability. Members or ex-members of Cambridge University were Tabs, and were considered by Oxonians to be beyond the pale, though they might, very occasionally, put up a decent sporting show in the Boat Race or a varsity match. Cricketing counties were referred to by abbreviations – Hants or Yorks – or adapted into weird forms, such as Wuggins and Gluggins. GB always referred to Northamptonshire as Polyglotshire, presumably because at one time it had several overseas players.

GB wearing a boater – from a video made from Eric Bowtell's films.

He had remarkable insights and remarkable capabilities. When I was in Middle Fourth, for one or two lessons a week he would teach us in Fifth Form Room together with Fifth Form, the scholarship form. We would be roughly two years below them, and how clear a lesson plan GB had I am not sure, but he gave us each his attention and never seemed to falter. Occasionally, the problems of one form would be referred to the other; and great was the glee when a Fourth-Former was able to correct one of his 'uncles' in Fifth Form.

Tim Miles, of the 1935 Fifth Form, wrote of GB:

> No words can adequately express what I owe to him, not only for his teaching but for his special consideration of one's individual needs; nothing was ever too much trouble. This is something which I have appreciated in retrospect perhaps more than I ever did at the time, though even then I am sure I recognised him as someone quite out of the ordinary. We were warned by GB against pedantic words such as 'commence' for 'begin' and 'succulent bivalve' for 'oyster'; his other dislikes were 'donation', 'spouse' and 'portion' (as in the café menu phrase '3d per portion'). On the strength of this some of us made up the following approximation to a Latin hexameter:
> 'He commenced to donate his spouse with a portion of succulent bivalve.'

My own memories of his lessons have him sitting at the end of a long table, around which the form would be ranged. Oral work had its place – particularly grammar and vocabulary tests – and marks would be entered as pencilled dots in his mark book. (I wonder if any of these survive?) Occasionally the hectoring manner would come through when one had forgotten something that one should have remembered: "Great Caesar's hatpin!" was a favourite cry, as was the incantation, "You hog, you dog, you lousy log, you leprous lump of cheese!"

He had a particular aversion to Peter Davies in my form: I don't know the history of this antipathy, but it was mutual. Years later and shortly before he died lamentably young, Peter became almost speechless with hatred when I questioned him about the matter. GB is also clear in my mind, spluttering with fury at some imagined enormity on Peter's part. On one occasion the spluttering resulted in his losing his false teeth, but with a sweeping gesture he collected them up and restored them to his mouth with hardly a pause in the invective. I never experienced the 'roots and tweaks' described by the actor Christopher Lee (see page 95), but tweaking and hair-pulling were common features of life at school: prefects were apparently allowed to give most unpleasant pain at the base of the spine with their knees, as well as pulling one's hair with extreme violence. This and the rotating brushes at Thomas's hairdresser's in Eton High Street may well account for the early loss of hair, including my own, in several generations.

One physical approach that GB did allow himself, however, was an extraordinary kneading of one's shoulder blade, which tickled like fury. In my memory, this usually took place while we were assembling bleary-eyed in Lower School before breakfast. It was genially meant, often being accompanied by some jocular remark. This sort of behaviour drew one of the bitterest memories of Summer Fields from an old boy, when Richard Usborne was trawling for impressions to include in *A Century of Summer Fields* (1964):

That was written by a man who had been at Summer Fields in 1940, when GB was in full swing and just starting to run the school while John Evans pottered amiably around the Study and the Farm. The war undoubtedly put a strain on both headmasters, and JFE (John Evans) had a breakdown in 1943. He was to have two more before he retired, and inevitably the burden of 'carrying on' fell upon GB. Other burdens added to the strain; he was a great stepper-into-breaches, but this and the Thames Valley climate took their toll. In 1960 he was ordered by his doctor not to spend another winter in Oxford, so he retired to Sussex, where he died four years later at the age of seventy. He just missed the centenary celebrations of the school to which he had devoted most of his life.

Here, then, is my attempt to weld GB's own memories with those that other people have of him. In doing so, I am aware that the realms of probability and the frontiers of fact may occasionally have been overstepped. Some aspects of GB stretch one's credulity, and it should be borne in mind that, in recalling his schooldays, no man is on oath: myths are absorbed, subscribed to and embroidered for the next generation. One of my friends, who had known GB, was horrified at the use of the word 'monster' in my title; but, having thought about it carefully, I do believe that he appeared a monster in the childhood sense to many young boys. He was no more nor less monstrous than the bull in the farm field, the ghost in the vestry, the many-headed hydra, or Goliath of Gath. Indeed, the boys of Cheam used to refer to him as 'Golgotha' (the hill of the skull). He bridged the gap between fact and fiction; so at times he was a myth, at times a monster, but Dr Jekyll was always waiting for his return to being a man. Perhaps the most intriguing question of all (and one which this study is unlikely to answer) is how aware GB was of the mythology which surrounded him. Did he play up to it, as many schoolmasters do? Did he come to think of himself, in Hollywood phrase, as a living legend? Probably not. Or (to quote the man himself) well, I'm not quite sure.

Nicholas Aldridge, Oxford, 2008.

Wilfred, GB and Joyce.

CHAPTER 1: BOYHOOD AND EDUCATION

GEOFFREY BOLTON was born on 30th July 1893, the year in which Wilfred Owen was born, the Independent Labour Party was founded, and Frederick Lanchester started to design his first motor car. GB was the eldest of five children born to Henry Bolton and his wife, Chloe, née Gordon. Henry was a notable London solicitor whose firm – Lee Bolton & Lee – was, and still is, situated at 1/2 The Sanctuary, next to Westminster Abbey.

The firm was founded by Henry's father, Thomas Bolton, in 1855, and was called simply Lee & Bolton before John Benjamin Lee's son, Henry Wilmot Lee, joined in 1874. J. B. Lee became legal secretary to the Archbishop of Canterbury, starting a connection which has lasted until today. Thomas Bolton managed the affairs of the Clergy Mutual Assurance Society and Queen Anne's Bounty.

Thomas's eldest son, Henry Lushington Bolton (his middle name came from his maternal grandmother, who was the granddaughter of the 1st Lord Harris), was taken on as a clerk in 1885, became a solicitor in 1890 and a partner in 1892. When his father died in 1895, Henry stepped into his shoes. He also inherited and developed the private practice of his father, and was for years responsible for the personal, as opposed to the official, affairs of many ecclesiastical dignitaries.

Henry Bolton tended to be rather annoyed by the dominant Lee presence, some of whose members may not have worked as hard as he did.

Henry Bolton (seated right) with the partners of Lee Bolton & Lee, c.1940.

"My father founded this firm," was a periodic comment of his, and it was partially true.

Probably at the time of GB's birth the family lived in London, at 57 Porchester Terrace, near Hyde Park, but in 1901 they moved to Crowborough in Sussex. Crowborough had become popular as a residential and dormitory town with the opening of the London railway in 1868. More importantly, in 1885 a Dr Charles Leeson Prince wrote a book praising its valetudinarian qualities and fine views; he distributed this throughout the country, and it led to an inundation of visitors. Many of these were so taken by the place that they stayed on to become permanent residents; this of course led to a boom in the building trade.

The Boltons bought a newly built house, The Gables on Beacon Road, for £3,000; the conveyance is dated 31st May 1901 and the house was bought in the name of Chloe. The family inhabited this house for twenty years, but in 1921, apparently finding it too small (even though most of the children had now left home), they moved down the road to a larger house in Goldsmith Avenue, possibly Gorsedene or Camperdown. The Gables had a large garden, including a croquet lawn and a vegetable garden, and over the years Chloe bought some adjoining land to enlarge it still further. The house's subsequent history is not without interest, as it was used in the Second World War to house workers at the King's Standing radio station in Ashdown Forest, which was the English equivalent of Lord Haw-Haw, broadcasting messages to discourage the Germans.

The Sanctuary: Lee Bolton & Lee.

The Gables, Crowborough.

Camperdown may have been briefly occupied by the Boltons in the early 1920s, but by the end of the decade the Straton-Ferriers lived there, as witness this photograph of the two boys, John and Brian, with the gardeners.

Once established in Crowborough, Henry worked in London all week, returning home on Saturday evenings; he was described by his younger daughter as a "dear little man", who was disappointed that none of his children followed him into his firm. The whole of his long life (he lived till 1948, having retired only two years previously, aged eighty-three) was devoted to the interests of his firm and its clients. He was a lovable and unselfish person, the embodiment of all that is best in a family solicitor, and he won the affection and confidence of his clients. Chloe was a very strong character and an avowed atheist. A beautiful portrait (painted by Nina Hardy in 1896) of her seated at her dressing table hung for many years on the wall of GB's room, and is now displayed on the staircase at Danny, the house to which he retired in 1960.

There is nothing to suggest that either of his parents was musical, but one did not necessarily have to be part of a musical household to pick up a passion for Gilbert and Sullivan. As Noel Coward, six years GB's junior, was to write in 1954:

> I was born into a generation that still took light music seriously. The lyrics and melodies of Gilbert and Sullivan were hummed and strummed into my consciousness at an early age. My father sang them, my mother played them, my nursemaid breathed them through her teeth while she was washing me, dressing me and undressing me and putting me to bed. My aunts and uncles, who were legion, sang them singly and in unison at the slightest provocation. By the time I was four years old, 'Take a Pair of Sparkling Eyes', 'Tit Willow' and 'I Have a Song to Sing-O' had been fairly inculcated into my bloodstream.

Whether or not GB had a similar early immersion in the Savoy Operas, he was

Chloe Bolton painted by Nina Hardy.

certainly a devotee of them by early manhood; though quite unmusical himself, he said that it was the music which particularly charmed him.

The other children after GB were Wilfred, who died young in the Dardanelles in June 1915; Joyce, who married but had no children; Richard, always known as Dick, who also had a childless marriage and became chairman of Bemax; and Angela, who was born in December 1910 and died in April 1993.

GB, Wilfred, Joyce and Dick.

GB begins his own *Recollections of Summer Fields* by recalling neighbours from the Crowborough days.

> Very near us at Crowborough lived the Rendel family. The two boys were much of an age with my brother and myself, so that during the holidays we saw a lot of one another. The Rendels were at Summer Fields, and it was then (in 1905 or 1906) that I first heard of that establishment and of the famous Dr Williams . . .

Herbert Rendel was born in 1894 and he was at Summer Fields in 1903–7; his brother Reginald was born in 1896 and he was at Summer Fields in 1907–9. In his reminiscences, *Kaleidoscope*, Herbert's son Guy mentions this connection, but believed mistakenly that GB had himself been a boy at Summer Fields.

26

In fact his prep school was the Grange in Crowborough, where he went in 1901 and where:

> cricket took precedence over everything else – so much so that, after four and a half years there, I knew much more of Wisden than I did of Kennedy or Abbott & Mansfield, and my indignant parents sent me elsewhere. Academically the move was a sound one, but cricket's chains were by then firmly riveted on me.

This was the first (unless preceded by Gilbert and Sullivan) and deepest love affair of GB's life; he was seldom a particularly impressive performer, but that did not diminish his intense adoration of the game, whether as spectator or player. His passion for it was nurtured by wide reading, and as a man he had a complete set of Wisden on his bookshelves.

His second prep school was Belmont in Brighton. It did a good job, for in a year and a half it brought him up to the standard where he was able to sit, and win, a scholarship to Repton. He entered P. G. Exham's house, The Orchard, in September 1907; it was quite common in those days for boys to enter their senior school at fourteen. Percy Exham was himself an Old Reptonian, and he had won an exhibition to St John's College, Cambridge, in 1880. He spent most of his working life (1883–1919) as a master at the school, teaching maths and having charge of The Orchard for twenty-two years from 1897; if that seems a long time, it may be noted that his predecessor was housemaster for forty years.

The Orchard, Repton.

The 1907 staff photo of Repton: Percy Exham is the portly moustached gentleman seated at the left end of the front row.

Exham was evidently a character – a burly man with a walrus moustache, as can be seen from the 1907 staff photograph. He had difficulty in staying awake – it is uncertain whether this was a sort of petit mal or some glandular condition. He was a good teacher and disciplinarian. A boy in his maths division who had been punished for bad work told his housemaster that he had not understood the problem.

"Why did you not ask Mr Exham to explain it again?" enquired the housemaster.

"Well, sir, he was asleep on a hat peg, and I did not like to disturb him."

GB spent the customary five years at the school, starting as a fag to H. S. Altham and ending his career as a house prefect. This period covered an important change in headmastership: in 1910, Lionel Ford, who had been headmaster since 1901, went on to take the reins at Harrow.

He was succeeded by William Temple, who was himself succeeded after only four years by Geoffrey Fisher (two consecutive archbishops of Canterbury!).

Lionel Ford.

William Temple.

Ford was a formidable headmaster, whose brief when he arrived in 1901 had been to restore the fortunes and good order to a school in decline. This he had done with firm discipline and a spate of new buildings. Some of his critics said that he was interested only in chapel and games; he was a fine cricketer from a cricketing family, and had taken holy orders while a master at Eton.

From the start, however, he stressed the importance of work in the classroom. He also introduced the system of school and house prefects. As *The Reptonian* explained:

There are fourteen school-prefects, chosen by the Headmaster, who are responsible for the order of the School at large . . . The prefect system is extended also to the houses, the Housemaster appointing one or more house-prefects in addition . . . to assist in maintaining order in the house. The house-prefects are rewarded for their labours by one shilling a week pocket money and by leave to stay up after prayers every night. The school-prefects have a still further honour, in that they are adorned with a speckled straw hat, ornamented with the School crest on the ribbon.

Ford expanded the school with a new boarding house, squash courts, a science school, a gymnasium, a swimming bath and an enlarged library. He increased the size of the chapel, too, and gave it a new organ. The 1900s also saw the reflowering of Repton cricket after a period of rather indifferent success in the late '90s, and in 1908 Altham was captain of a fine eleven, which has been called "the best cricket team that has ever taken the field for any school". He topped the batting averages (as he had done in the previous year, too) and also led The Orchard to victory in the inter-house competition. If his fag needed any further stimulus in his love affair with cricket, this would surely have provided it. The setting was perfect: a lovely school with a good spirit, taking its work seriously, but putting almost as much devotion into watching on those long, sunny half-holidays as the heroes of the XI trounced Uppingham by ten wickets. Indeed, it is not fanciful to believe that public schoolboys of those days, glutted as they were on the classics, saw something fine and Homeric in their school matches. It was presumably Repton that gave GB his love of Homer, and Oxford that reinforced it. He was made a Foundation Scholar in the summer of 1909.

C. B. Fry.

The Repton 1st XI, 1908. Harry Altham as captain sits in the middle of the middle row.

GB was a great and self-confessed hero-worshipper. His most obvious heroes were those in the world of cricket, notably three Oxonians, two of whom were also Reptonians.

When he arrived at Repton, the older generation would no doubt still be singing the praises of Charles Burgess Fry, who had been in the cricket XI for four years, 1888–91. Captain in 1890 and 1891, he had a batting average of nearly fifty in his final year. Repton had a reputation for the excellence of its cricket in the early 1890s, and Fry was a source of inspiration to the subsequent successful players. He grew to be a remarkable man as well as a fine athlete and cricketer. He went on from Repton to Wadham College, Oxford, where he captained the university at both cricket and soccer, and was ultimately captain of Sussex and of England. He broke the world long-jump record in 1892, and was at one stage nearly offered the crown of Albania (it was perhaps as well for him that the offer never quite materialised!). Fry seems generally to have been referred to by his initials, rather than as Charles Fry: could this have been what impelled GB to adopt a similar style?

Quite apart from his brilliance in the sporting world, Fry was a man of great culture and width of interests. He gained a first in Classical Honour Mods at Oxford, stood as a Liberal candidate for Brighton, and for forty years with his wife ran the training ship *Mercury* on the River Hamble, where he inculcated classical values to growing young men. He also wrote widely about cricket and other topics, editing a monthly magazine and producing a book, *Cricket: Batsmanship*, which, as Neville Cardus so pithily put it, "might conceivably have come from the pen of Aristotle, had Aristotle lived now and played cricket".

If Fry was one of GB's role models, so more immediately was Harry Altham, head of The Orchard and head prefect of Repton in GB's first year there. As has been said, his final cricket season as captain was a splendid one, and he topped the batting averages for the second time. He was a stylish opening bat, and also bowled useful lobs – one sometimes forgets that, even in the early years of the twentieth century, lob-bowling was current – but when he went on to Oxford with an exhibition to Trinity College, he developed a medium-slow overarm delivery.

Subsequently, he played briefly for Surrey – mainly with their second XI. His only first-class appearance was against Leicestershire at the Oval in 1908; yes, a public-schoolboy playing for a county, like the Jackson brothers in P. G. Wodehouse's *Mike*. From 1913, Altham's loyalties lay with Hampshire, but the war interrupted his early career with them. He was commissioned in the 60th Rifles (the King's Royal Rifle Corps), and served for four years in France, ending as a major, DSO and MC and thrice mentioned in despatches. He made his debut for Hampshire in 1919 and played sporadically for them from 1921 to 1923.

He belonged to a plethora of the amateur cricket clubs that were such a feature of life between the wars: MCC, Free Foresters, Harlequins, I Zingari, Cryptics, Hampshire Hogs, Authentics, etc. GB would no doubt have kept in touch with him when these clubs played the Sussex Martlets or Oxford. But it was as a teacher that Altham is equally remembered, being on the Winchester staff for thirty years. He was master in charge of cricket, 1929–33, and a housemaster, 1927–47. He was treasurer of the MCC, 1950–63, and he was instrumental in founding the MCC Youth Cricket Association, of which he was chairman, 1952–65. In 1954 he was chairman of the England selectors, and president of MCC, 1959–60. He and Martin Donnelly shared the dedication of GB's *History of the O.U.C.C.*

GB himself did not scale the heights of achievement in cricket; he was sometimes picked for the house XI in his last summer, but he was not included in the team which beat Brook House in the final. Indeed, his name features but seldom in the sporting sections of *The Reptonian*; he does, however, appear frequently in the School Debates in his two senior years.

By this time William Temple had become headmaster. He was a young man of twenty-eight, a novice to schoolmastering and a great contrast to Ford – one might say an Athenian following a Corinthian. His main influence was on the intellectual life of the school, though he did build a new cricket pavilion. His discipline was less stern, but he had 'a deep and completely spontaneous love for the boys', as D. C. Somervell later wrote:

> He simply delighted in their boyishness; they knew it and responded. I do not believe there ever was another Headmaster who gave his school quite this and to quite the same extent . . .
>
> And, secondly, he offered to those who could appreciate it the keys to the splendid storehouse of his intellectual powers – in scholarship, in theology, in literature and art and current affairs; his sermons; his expositions of Plato, of Aeschylus, of Shakespeare, of Browning; he did not play down to those he taught; he took them intellectually by the scruff of the neck and drew them towards himself. He was Oxford come to Repton.

GB's maiden speech was made on 4th October 1910, defending Robert Blatchford on a charge of endangering the safety, honour and welfare of His Majesty's dominions by his pamphlets and articles.

Mr BOLTON then rose for the Defence, calm but indignant. Mr Anderson was totally wrong in his facts about Germany. That country would certainly invade France, for the purpose of retaining her hold on Alsace-Lorraine, and gaining Cherbourg and Brest as naval bases.

This she could easily do, and overrun Holland and Belgium as well, for England had no army worth speaking of, and the French one was notoriously disorganised (cries of dissent from the audience); besides this Russia would undoubtedly remain neutral.

As for the pamphlet, Lord Roberts himself wrote pamphlets on the subject, and Lord Charles Beresford's views were much the same. Mr Blatchford was a strong-minded man who did not mind speaking out his opinions. Could he be blamed for this? Mr Bolton's disgust at the bare idea overpowered him, and he sat down amid prolonged applause.

The defence was victorious by thirty-nine votes to six.

GB appeared again on Thursday 1st December, the motion being that 'Members of Parliament should be paid a salary sufficient for their maintenance while acting as such'.

In a debate on the nationalisation of the railways on Thursday 2nd February, he considered that the success of the post office was due to Mr Sydney Buxton (of whom he said many complimentary things) rather than to the state.

A month later, he was a leading speaker, proposing the motion that 'This house disapproves of music halls'.

Mr BOLTON considered that Music Halls kept clerks away from healthy outdoor enjoyments on Saturday afternoons. There were some very low-class Music Halls. The speaker had never visited them, but thought that the mere fact of their being situated in Houndsditch, Shoreditch, Bethnal Green &c., proved that they were far from refined. At the better-class Music Halls the latter half of the programme was often good. But the beginning part was generally very childish and horrible. He did not approve of classical dancing – it was often overdone and at times indecent. He could hardly expect a very high standard from the provincial Music Halls. Some indeed – the Brighton Aquarium in particular – were positively revolting. Such being the case, Mr Bolton, though he admitted that there was some prospect of brighter times in the future, could not refrain from heartily disapproving of the present-day Music Hall.

The motion lost by twenty-one votes to thirty-three. A very successful debate came to a close amidst cheers and boos.

In the following debating season, GB spoke on several occasions, and on 30th November he opposed the motion that 'This house disapproves of the action of those who voted against the Parliament Bill in the House of Lords', carrying the day, as the motion was defeated by twenty-six votes to eleven.

On 1st February 1912, there was a debate that 'Immediate war with Germany is eminently desirable' (alas, regardless of their doom, the little victims debate!):

Mr BOLTON referred to a certain toast drunk in German military circles, emphasised the necessity of stopping German trade, and informed the House that Germany must be crushed.

In a debate on 29th February about the urgent need to reform public schools, GB was very angry at the assertion that no leader in any form of national activity was a public-school man, and cited Mr Asquith as an example. He also signified his bitter contempt for racquets.

> Mr Oddy, Mr Bolton, Mr Crommelin Brown and Mr Somervell then indulged in a little chat on the relative popularity of cricket and racquets at Winchester, Eton and Harrow.

This foreshadows GB's later contempt for tennis.

His finest hour came as proposer on 15th February (possibly a misprint for March) of the motion that 'This house considers that Home Rule for Ireland would be a disaster', his second opponent being the headmaster. He gave what was described as 'an excellent partizan[sic] speech'. There was a record attendance at this debate of 140 from the school and twenty visitors; the motion was carried by 107 to thirty-three in what was, according to the secretary, 'one of the most successful debates we have ever attended'.

In his final summer, GB played for his house 2nd XI, making fifty not out for Exham's v Surtees' and taking six for twenty against The Hall (L-Z). In the first round of the senior house matches he made six in each innings against Stratton's and held two catches but was not put on to bowl. In the semi-final, again batting tenth, he made one and two not out. Though Exham's were victorious, he was not included in the final, which they also won. He left as a house prefect and a member of the upper sixth in July. It had been a good summer in events but not in weather. Here is an excerpt from *History of the O.U.C.C.*, which he wrote in the late fifties:

> 1912. This was the summer of the first and only Triangular Tournament and was a summer which for sheer frightfulness was not equalled until 1956. *Punch* had a cartoon of England, Australia and South Africa sheltering under umbrellas and singing:
>
> > "When shall we three meet again,
> > In thunder, lightning or in rain?"

GB went up to University College, Oxford, in 1912, to read Greats – the popular name for *Literae Humaniores*, a classical course lasting for four years and divided into two sections. His rooms were in Kitchen Staircase 7 – nothing very special – but he was content enough to stay in them a second year. After he had sat Mods (in which he gained a modest third), however, the Great War intervened. He never went on to complete his degree; but, like his contemporaries at the college, he was automatically awarded a BA in 1916, which he then converted to an MA in 1919. This was done on the assumption that these undergraduates would have got a degree in the end, and it ensured the college wasn't swamped by people returning to finish their degrees when the war ended. So, though he did get a full degree, it was never an honours one.

He had joined the Royal Sussex Regiment as a territorial in 1913; and next year the Archduke Franz Ferdinand took his fatal trip to Serbia.

THE TRIANGULAR FARCE.

Scene—*A blasted pitch.*

Chorus. "WHEN SHALL WE THREE MEET AGAIN
IN THUNDER, LIGHTNING OR IN RAIN?"

Punch *cartoon, April 1912.*

University College, Oxford.

CHAPTER 2: WAR

IT IS AN ODD REFLECTION [GB wrote in his memoirs] that a bomb thrown at Sarajevo in 1914 should have led (among other consequences) to my becoming Headmaster of Summer Fields in 1956. For when I was home from France in 1915, I was posted to the reserve battalion of the Cinque Ports, and there (at Woolwich, I think, or some other ghastly spot) I first met Geoffrey Alington. It did not take us long to discover that we had practically everything in common: a love of Oxford, the Classics, cricket, Gilbert and Sullivan; a knowledge-by-heart of much of the works of Wodehouse, A. A. Milne, Kipling, Hornung, Anthony Hope; and a hearty dislike of our C.O. and most of his senior officers, not one of whom had the slightest intention of going to the front.

Geoffrey Hugh Alington was the eldest of the four sons of Edward Hugh Alington and his wife, Margaret. She was the younger daughter of Archibald and Gertrude Maclaren, who founded Summer Fields, their elder daughter, Mabel, having married Dr Charles Williams. On the death of Mrs Maclaren in 1896, Dr Williams took over the school with Hugh Alington (known to all at Summer Fields as 'the Bear') as his partner, running the games and the senior boarding house, Mayfield. The Bear succeeded to the headmastership in 1917, though the Doctor retained much of the financial control of the school.

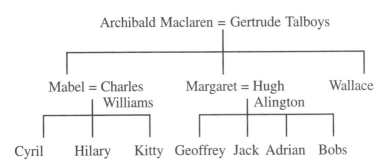

Geoffrey Alington adored schoolmastering. He involved himself in all aspects of school life, having been a scholar at Marlborough, a devoted classicist and a keen cricketer, despite poor eyesight which meant he had to wear spectacles. As a boy, he had been at Horris Hill (in many ways the friendliest of Summer

Field's rivals) and had made 109 not out in a 2nd XI match between the two schools. He was an enthusiastic producer and writer of plays for the boys, three of which were published in 1913. His mind remained very much on Summer Fields; he had taught there for three years, and then for two years before the war at its daughter school, Summer Fields St Leonard's in Sussex. He even composed Latin proses in the trenches and sent them back for the boys to do; it is not recorded whether the boys were grateful for this, but no doubt Geoffrey was a great hero to them.

The other three Alington sons were also involved in some way with the school. Jack (who was possibly a bit simple) was, for a while at least, unofficial bursar; Adrian was the only one to attend Summer Fields as a pupil (1904–8), and he later wrote a brilliant prep-school novel, *Chaytors*, which draws heavily on Summer Fields and its inhabitants; and Bobs, the youngest, taught at the school from 1922 to 1937, being a partner during the 1930s before he left to become an Inspector of Schools.

Geoffrey Alington.

It may be that having a common Christian name cemented the bond, though GB was not 'Geoffrey' to many. Of Alington he writes:

Geoffrey was quite wonderful with the troops. He loathed war even more than I did, but he had a real flair for dealing with the men. He was for ever trying to organize entertainments for them and I suspect that he was the confidant of many of them. As it turned out, our friendship had one aspect that was vitally important to me, for Geoffrey proved to be the son of the about-to-be headmaster of Summer Fields. Naturally, we discussed schoolmastering a lot. At the end of two years at Oxford I had not decided what I wanted to do, though I rather hankered after being a schoolmaster.

Geoffrey's whole being was bound up in Summer Fields. At that time I believe the arrangement was that he should run the Oxford school with his cousin Hilary (Williams), the Doctor's younger son, while Cyril Williams (the elder) would take over at St Leonard's. I soon made up my mind that I should like to go to Summer Fields, and Geoffrey acquiesced. I think that he must have mentioned it to his parents quite early on. At any rate, Mrs Alington, whom I first met in that summer of 1915, always talked to me (and later wrote to me) as if she knew all about the plan.

GB was always reticent about his own war, but a certain amount can be gleaned from other sources. One story he did tell, though. All junior officers were ordered to stop shaving the upper lip area. Hairy or hairless, it did not matter: the order was to grow a moustache, and this continued until it was discovered that the Prince of Wales could not grow one. So the order was cancelled, to the great delight of GB and others.

He had been commissioned as a 2nd lieutenant in the Territorials in April 1913; this is referred to in Battalion Orders: '5th (Cinque Ports) Battalion, the Royal Sussex Regiment. Geoffrey Bolton (late Cadet Corporal, Repton School Contingent, Junior Division, Officers Training Corps) to be Second Lieutenant. Dated 12 April 1913.' The 5th Battalion had mediaeval origins and was the descendant of the three battalions raised by William Pitt as Lord Warden of the Cinque Ports to face the threatened Napoleonic invasion in 1803. They also fought in the Boer War, and at the beginning of the twentiethth century were known as 'Brookfield's Greys' after Lieutenant Colonel Brookfield, the MP for Rye and their commanding officer. In 1911 this post was taken on by Lieutenant Colonel F. G. Langham. He was photographed with his officers at the 1913 annual camp, held on the Ladies' Mile at Patcham near Brighton, from 27th July to 10th August.

GB among officers at Patcham, sitting cross-legged, second left.

Summer Fields' extended family, the ruling dynasty of Maclarens, Williamses and Alingtons, here assembled on 4th August 1905 for Cyril Williams' twenty-first birthday. This picture includes friends as well as relations, and many are unidentified, starting with the whole of the top row, except for Geoffrey Alington, who is third from left. After that it is easier. The second row from the top is: Mrs Gmelin, Revd C. H. S. Gmelin, then three unknowns, Ethel Maclaren, T. J. F. Haskoll, Mrs Haskoll, G. W. Evans (Bam), J. F. Crofts (Crab) and one more unknown.

The third row is: Wallace Maclaren*, unidentified large man, a grandmother figure – possibly Dr Williams' mother(?), Revd C. E. Williams (the Doctor), Mabel Williams, Cyril Williams, Margaret Alington, Wallace Maclaren*, Revd E. H. Alington (the Bear). On the ground: ...cil Maclaren, unknown, Hilary Williams, Kitty Williams, Jack Alington, unknown, 'Bobs' Alington, Archibald Maclaren. (* I have hedged my bets on Wallace Maclaren, with two possibilities!)

Next year's camp was at Bordon, and during it things began to hot up, as was later described in the *Cinque Ports Gazette*:

> On Sunday 26th July, the Battalion went into Camp at Bordon, and on 30th set out on the divisional march [to Salisbury Plain – this was apparently the first time that a Territorial division had been called upon to undertake a divisional march, and sceptics predicted a debacle, but the battalion came through remarkably well]. On that Wednesday the troops of the Surrey Brigade, to which the Cinque Ports Battalion was attached, marched in two columns to Chawton, one mile south of Alton. During the previous day, all ranks became aware of something unusual in the air by the declaration of 'Precautionary Period', which automatically brought into operation the Special Service Sections of three officers and thirty-five other ranks, which had for some years been trained for special duties in those Territorial Battalions contiguous to the coast.
>
> These had been organised to work in conjunction with the Coast Guard Stations which, on 'Precautionary Period' being declared, automatically became 'War Signal Stations'. No small sensation was caused, therefore, when that same evening the Special Service Section of the Cinque Ports marched off amidst enthusiastic cheers under Lieutenant R. M. Pope, with Lieutenant G. Bolton and 2/Lieut. R. Fazan, for their War Station in the Dover Defences.

GB standing extreme left, with other officers at the Tower of London.

GB was promoted to full lieutenant in August 1914. The battalion spent the first months of the war at Dover Castle, where GB must have carried out garrison duties and helped to train recruits and reservists. From 16th October 1914, the battalion was at the Tower of London, assuming the role of a Guards battalion. They would have performed duties such as the nightly Ceremony of the Keys and the Bank Picquet. They also lined the streets for the State Opening of Parliament and escorted and guarded the spy, Carl Hans Lody, who was executed in the Tower.

Four months later, on 18th February, they embarked on SS *Pancras* at Southampton for France, arriving at Le Havre on the following day. GB was listed as an officer with "D" Company, which had been amalgamated from the "G" (Crowborough) and "H" (Ore) companies during preparations for active service.

After Ypres, Territorial battalions reinforced the depleted regular brigades, and the 5th Battalion joined the 2nd Royal Sussex Regiment in the 2nd Brigade of the 1st Division of the Old Contemptibles. They were in reserve for the Battle of Neuve Chapelle, which began on 10th March, and they first went into the front line, at Richebourg l'Avoué, on the 27th.

In April the battalion was hit by a measles epidemic, and over the next month some hundred of its members were struck down, many being invalided home to England. GB was admitted to No. 1 Field Ambulance Station with measles on 20th April, while the battalion was at rest in billets at Gonnehem near Richebourg St Vaast. Next day he was moved to No. 4 Casualty Clearing Station at Lillers, and on 5th May he was invalided home on the hospital ship *St Patrick*. Four days later, his battalion suffered heavy losses at Aubers Ridge. He seems to have spent most of the summer back in England, and it was during this time, as explained above, that he first met Geoffrey Alington.

Some of his possessions from the war have recently come to light: half a dozen maps, the officer's stand-by, the *Field Service Pocket Book*, and a notepad called A.B. 153[B] from which several sheets have been torn, but some remain. Mostly they are lists or sets of instructions; two pages, however, are in the nature of a diary, which is intriguing but tantalising:

Fri. Sept. 17.	Left Windsor for Southampton. Spent night at Dolphin Hotel.
Sat. 18.	Went on board SS. Hantonia [?]
Sun. 19. in	Crossed early to France. Went to Hotel Normandie. Entrained evening for Rouen.
Mon. 20.	Arr. Rouen early, went to No 1. T.B.D. Spent afternoon in Rouen.
Tue. 21.	Morning: Instruction in M.G. Lewis Gun. Aft: Left Rouen i/c drafts for S. Lancs & Monmouths. Night in train.
Wed. 22.	Arr. Acheux in afternoon & disposed of drafts. Rejoined Regt. at Sailly au Bois. 6 p.m. went back to D Coy.
Sep. 27th.	D Coy went to dug-outs about ½ mile behind the line.
Oct. 4th.	Relieved from dug-outs & back to billets.
" 7th.	Took out night working party.

And that is all that there is.

At this time, GB was promoted to temporary captain, but this promotion apparently did not become operative as another captain arrived from England; in fact, GB was not promoted to captain until May 1917. When he rejoined them in 1915, the 5th had become a pioneer battalion with Major General Fanshawe's 48th (South Midland) Division, composed entirely of Territorials.

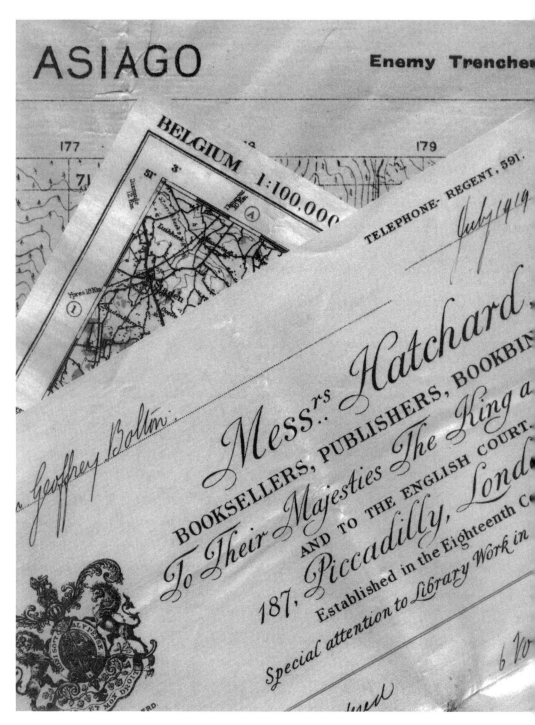

ASIAGO

Enemy Trenche[s]

BELGIUM 1:100,000

TELEPHONE- REGENT, 591.

July 1919

Geoffrey Bolton

Messrs Hatchard,

BOOKSELLERS, PUBLISHERS, BOOKBIN[DERS]

To Their Majesties The King a[nd]

AND TO THE ENGLISH COURT.

187, Piccadilly, Lond[on]

Established in the Eighteenth C[entury]

Special attention to Library Work in

GB, a voracious reader, kept an account at Hatchard's throughout the war.

44

Pioneer battalions were new to the British Army, being a combination of infantry and engineers. As pioneers, the 5th Battalion took part in the Battle of the Somme in 1916 and the 3rd Battle of Ypres in 1917. But GB himself missed the Somme. He was admitted to hospital on 15th June 1916 and was transferred to England a week later; the Battle of the Somme began on 1st July. One can only speculate as to what this second illness was. Could he have been gassed badly enough to need hospitalisation and repatriation, but not badly enough to prevent his being a regular smoker for the rest of his life? The alternative is shell-shock, that elusive complaint (but no doubt only too real to its sufferers) which struck many in this war and affected their subsequent lives. Was this the basis for part of the GB myth?

Hilary Williams was killed at Loos in 1915, and Geoffrey Alington was killed a year later at Bouzincourt. He had just returned from the trenches and settled his men in billets when a shell burst in front of the chair in which he was resting in the garden. Shortly before his death he had helped to launch the *Cinque Ports Gazette*, an 'active service magazine for all ranks of the 5th Royal Sussex Regiment'. It first appeared in May 1916, and only ran to three issues,[1] the second of which mentions that GB bowled 'with considerable effect' in a cricket match for "D" Company against the battalion's Lewis gunners. The third issue included a moving tribute to Alington by the editor:

> No officer in the Battalion was more liked or respected. The soul of good humour, many were the times when his cheeriness had helped to chase gloom away. He was one of the originators of the Gazette and had worked hard and untiringly to make it a success. He took the keenest interest in his men, and on many occasions arranged concerts or got up cricket and football matches in which he showed the same qualities which made him so successful an officer. His death came as a tremendous shock to us all.

GB, however, survived.

> With my usual luck, I fell seriously ill just before the opening of the Somme battle and was sent back to England. My last sight of Geoffrey was as I left in the ambulance; he was sitting on a ration-cart, having just returned from leave, and was looking the picture of misery. While I was recovering, he wrote and suggested that I should go and stay with his parents; and so at last I came to Summer Fields, or rather to Mayfield, where the Alingtons then lived.

That visit was memorable not only for meeting the Alingtons. GB went down to Somerville, which was being used as a convalescent hospital for officers, to see a wounded officer of his regiment. This officer introduced him to 'John Evans, the cricketer', and thus it was that the two future headmasters of Summer Fields first met. But tragedy was at hand. At the end of his visit, as he was waiting for his taxi, Mr Alington came up and told him that they had just heard of Geoffrey's death in action.

GB became devoted to the Alingtons.

John Evans, far right.

Margaret and 'Bear' Alington.

Mrs Alington (Aunt Margaret) was a wonderful mother and a wonderful wife for a headmaster. Although almost totally deaf, she knew everything that was going on, she knew the boys inside out and she 'had a way with her,' as they say, which endeared her not only to parents but to all with whom she came in contact. Because I had been Geoffrey's friend, she wrote to me regularly for the rest of the war, and as soon as I got home she invited me to Summer Fields, where she and her husband had succeeded Dr and Mrs Williams in 1917.

As a result of his second illness, GB was posted to the 4th (Territorial) Reserve Battalion, Royal Sussex, a home-based training unit, by order of a medical board, with effect from 10th November 1916. His return to the 5th Battalion appears to have been via the 8th Battalion, which was another pioneer unit. He rejoined "D" Company on 29th June 1917, and presumably therefore took part in the 3rd Battle of Ypres, in which the battalion was involved a month later.

The battalion ended the war in Italy, as is witnessed by a map of the Asiago area among GB's effects and a reference in the *Cinque Ports Gazette* of June 1932. It features a photograph of a group of officers of the battalion taken in Italy at the end of the war. 'Unfortunately, a good many officers who were then serving with the Battalion were absent from the group . . . Thus, Capt. Geoffrey Bolton was Town Major at Fara.' This was early in 1919, and shortly after that he was demobilised and headed for home and Summer Fields, where a job was evidently awaiting him.

Directly after lunch on the day of my arrival, I was taken to the Study by Hugh Alington – hereafter to be called Uncle Hugh – given a cigar and a copy of the rules of bracketing and underlining,[2] and told that I might, if I wished, consider myself engaged as a master as from the following September. Had I been demobilized a week earlier, I should probably have joined in May. But then I should have missed that glorious summer term of 1919 when Oxford cast off her mourning and returned with surprising speed to something like her old self.

Those of us who had spent a year or two at Oxford before the war and were lucky enough to return there imagined – or so it seemed in retrospect – that we were returning to the Oxford of 1914 and we did our best to make it so. Never mind whether or not we were right or wrong; that was the prevailing mood. We were anxious to enjoy ourselves again. For those whose enjoyments included watching cricket the O.U.C.C., desperate for funds, made things easy. Before the war it would have been a Liberty for the ordinary member of his College side to join the Varsity cricket club and, as far as I know, nobody of less than Authentics rank ever did. After the war we were besought to join – and we joined in droves. Watching cricket from the pavilion is far more fun than watching it from the ropes, as we were quick to appreciate. Memory can be deceptive, but as one looks back it seems that in 1919 the pavilion was always full.

Understanding that I should have to teach Maths, a subject of which I was abysmally ignorant, I thought I had better engage a tutor – which would give me a grand excuse for a return to Oxford. So I hired George Wood of Magdalen College School, a lifelong friend, as it turned out, of most of the Summer Fields masters. With him I did three hours a week; *for* him perhaps another three. Which left plenty of time for six days' cricket a week.

At Lord's, one day in May, GB ran into Asa Thomas, a doyen of the Sussex Martlets, from whom he heard that G. V. Campbell was trying to raise a side to play at Lancing in July. He lost no time in signing up for the game, and so, as he puts it, 'at Lancing we duly opened the second phase of the Martlets' history with a handsome win over the school'.

Years later, when GB was president of the Sussex Martlets, he wrote a history of the club to coincide with its golden jubilee in 1955. It had begun when, in 1905, the old Gentlemen of Sussex club came to an end, and a band of enthusiasts decided to found a club 'to encourage amateur cricket and to give members an opportunity of playing in the County of Sussex'. Membership was confined to university or public-school men and officers (past or present) in HM Forces. Early members included Sir Arthur Conan Doyle, Ranjitsinhji and GB's Reptonian hero, C. B. Fry.

His short history has many characteristic touches. 'In its early years the Club was known, rather clumsily, as the Hove Long Vacation Club, but in 1907 the far more appropriate title of the Sussex Martlets was adopted.' A martlet is the heraldic version of a martin or swallow. Its connection with Sussex seems to lie in the punning coat of arms of the de Arundel family, which is usually blazoned sable six swallows argent (the French for a swallow being *hirondelle*).

Martlet – Hirondelle – *Arundel.*

K. S. Ranjitsinhji.

GB goes on to say:

Ranji is known to have played at least once for the Club, but the match cannot be traced. In those happy days three things only were required of a Prep. School master – a University degree, a knowledge of the Latin grammar and an ability to play cricket – and this list [of early playing members] shows how well the Sussex schools were stocked.

Perhaps the greatest contrast between those days and these is to be found in the number of fixtures. For 1955 the Martlets have some 60 games arranged; in 1913, there were but 10 or 11! Matches against the Sussex Public Schools were then, as now, a feature of the programme, but of other pre-1914 opponents only the Blue Mantles survive. Country House matches [and here we dive straight into the world of Raffles], such as those against Sir Jeremiah Colman's XI at Reigate, have gone the way of the Country Houses, and, pace the new democracy, none is the better for their going. On the other hand, the greatly increased number of Old Boy tours and tours by Oxford and Cambridge Colleges have caused welcome additions to our fixtures. Games with the Cryptics and the United Services are of long standing, but do not seem to have been played regularly before 1919.

That year, GB played for the Sussex Martlets against the Cryptics; he was bowled for six by A. E. R. Gilligan, who was to captain England from 1924 to 1925. GB was later to join the Cryptics himself: the club had been founded in 1910 and it played, and invariably beat, the Summer Fields staff before the war.

It was during the summer of 1919 that GB first met Dr Williams, who had ceased to be headmaster but still controlled the finances and policies of the school. It so happened that Dr and Mrs Williams went to stay at Crowborough in September, just in time to stop GB as he was setting off for Summer Fields. Nobody had told him that the summer holidays had been extended by a week to celebrate the end of the war.

Summer Fields, Near Oxford, School House.

Notes:

1. That is, during the war. It was revived again in 1930, and appeared through the thirties until 1939. It is from this later edition that we learn a little of GB's movements in Italy.
2. This was a complicated system for tackling Latin or Greek translation. All subordinate clauses were bracketed and all words which agreed together were underlined. L. A. G. Strong considered that it produced accurate but pedestrian translation.

Summer Fields, Near Oxford, 1st. Game Cricket Ground.

Summer Fields, Near Oxford, The Gymnasium.

The masters, 1921. (Standing) 'Liz' Lysaght, L. A. G. Strong, GB, Billy Case, Bryan Buckley; (seated) F. P. Penny, Revd E. H. Alington, 'Bam' Evans; (on the ground) Ralph Robinson, John Evans, C. E. Smyth.

CHAPTER 3: SUMMER FIELDS

SUMMER FIELDS, when GB joined the teaching staff, had recently had a change of headmaster – in name, at any rate. Dr Williams, who had been in charge since before the death of Mrs Maclaren in 1896, had handed over the day-to-day running of the school to his brother-in-law Hugh Alington, but still to a large extent held the reins. There was, too, a welcome influx of new blood now that the war was over. John Evans had returned in the summer, and in September GB was one of three more arrivals, the other two being E. K. Barber, the Williams' son-in-law, who had been on the staff for five terms before the war, and the Hon. B. B. Buckley, who was an old boy of the school; so GB was in a sense the only new boy.

And he felt it. One may make allowance for the habitual self-deprecation in his memoirs, but even so the assembled staff must have been daunting.

> I had been during the war in many officers' messes where the inhabitants were strangers to me, but I had never been so overwhelmed with shyness and stage-fright as I was now. Besides the Alingtons and John Evans, I had met Cyril Williams and his wife and Kitty Barber, but the rest of the assembly fairly petrified me: they looked so terribly efficient and grim. They *were* efficient, too, but much less grim than I thought.
>
> The conversation at dinner was largely shop, and what could I know of that? I felt that the end had come when, after dinner, Lysaght backed me into a corner and asked me for my views on how to teach History. Dear Liz always swore in after-years that he could have done no such thing. But he did!

J. A. C. Lysaght, known as Liz and revealed as a clergyman by his collar (though he wore it only on official occasions), was one of the two middle-aged members of the teaching staff, the other being W. S. Case, the music master. The old brigade, apart from the Doctor and the Bear, was led by J. F. Crofts and G. W. Evans, who had both done more than thirty-five years. Then came F. P. Penny and C. E. Smyth. The aura and characters of these sages are depicted in the autobiography of L. A. G. Strong, who came to Summer Fields two years before GB and stayed until 1930.

> Billy Case will be talked about as long as two people who knew him are alive. Music was in his blood; his second name, Sterndale, came from Sterndale Bennett, his maternal grandfather. The other side of his background was

academic: his father, Thomas Case, had been Principal of Corpus.

Tommy Case was also the author of a verse epitaph on Gladstone, which GB quotes in his memoirs:

> Here lie I: until this last time
> Lying has been my favourite pastime.
> Lord, send me to the heavenly choir,
> Where I may ever play the lyre.

Apparently, the Liberal paper which had advertised for epitaphs upon the Grand Old Man did not award this effort the prize.

The senior assistant master, J. F. Crofts, lean, with a grizzled beard and rheumy eyes, must have been well into his sixties. Next came one Evans, an Irishman who taught French in a broad Dublin accent; affable and learned in a haphazard way, he played obsequious second fiddle to Crofts. He was known to the boys as Bam, a monosyllable of obscure derivation which, like most school nicknames, perfectly suited his appearance and personality. There was another Irishman on the staff, Cecil Smyth. Aged round fifty, he was of insignificant but slightly horsy appearance, had a smoker's cough and made no secret of his contempt for those above him. I received from him a great deal of shrewd advice on teaching and much brusque kindness.

Frederick Prescott Penny, Ping-Pong to his pupils, was a little, active, dry, spare man with a moustache which jutted out whenever he was indignant or incommoded. He sang tenor in the choir, voted Tory, and could be relied on to take the conventional view of any topic. Agreeable, kind-hearted, a small martinet, he taught in a series of clichés, which the boys quickly learned and afterwards remembered with affection.

Of all these the strongest personality was Case. Trained for the profession of music in England and Germany, he had been an assistant music critic on *The Times*. He reviewed, he wrote verse, he composed, and then, finding the late hours of musical journalism bad for his digestion, he took up schoolmastering. He was also a fine cricketer, playing for the Authentics and I Zingari. In all he did, he was handicapped by heart trouble; it was not so bad as to debar him from leading a reasonably active life, but he needed to take care. He had no self-consciousness, and would gambol with the smaller boys in a way that sometimes excited the derision of the older; but no one took liberties with him, for, if provoked, he could command sarcasm of a kind no boy can stand up to.

GB was soon on good terms with Strong and shared his admiration of Case. With these and the younger element – John Evans, Ken Barber and Bryan Buckley – he set about making the place more human.

On arrival, I was taken to Front Lodge, which was to be my home for the next twenty years. I had not expected a sitting-room of my own, even though I was to share this with Bryan Buckley. We did in fact share it for six years until he married, and I doubt if we exchanged a cross word in all that time. Later in the evening I remember Cyril Williams and C. E. Smyth coming to our room and telling us where we should have to take our forms. Nobody knew whether or not there would be a school, as one of those railway strikes which were such a feature of post-war years occurred on the very day that the boys were due back.

Front Lodge.

Actually, something less than twenty boys arrived. Among these, GB was pleased to identify Neville Ford, whom he had last seen in his pram at Repton. The Bear annexed the Fifth Form boys, and the rest of the staff took it in turn to teach the others. It was an unusual start to a teaching career. Breakfast was at 9 a.m. and there was little attempt at co-ordinated work or games. Gradually more boys returned and GB began to put names to faces. Finally, when the school was assembled, a normal timetable was resumed.

It was a demanding programme. Breakfast (preceded by prayers in New Room) was at 7.45; at 8.40 masters did five minutes of physical exercises with the form that they were going to take at 8.45. Morning school lasted from 8.45 to 1.30 with a forty-five-minute break at 10.45. Lunch at 1.30 was followed by games at 2.30; afternoon school was from 4 to 6; tea was at 6 (the masters then dining in the junior form rooms known as the Miss Hills' Rooms); chapel was at 7.10; and prep was from 7.30 to 8.30. Perhaps GB was lucky in having Wednesday, a half-holiday, as his duty day. A full programme in school *plus* being on duty during the rest of the day was quite something.

SUMMER FIELDS.

Hour.	Monday.	Tuesday.	Wednesday.	Thursday.	Friday.	Saturday.
1st 8·45 — 9·45	Greek	Greek	Maths	Greek	Greek	Maths
2nd 9·45 – 10·45	Latin	Latin	French	Latin	Latin	French
3rd 11·30 — 12·30	Maths	Maths	Latin Verses	Maths	Maths	Latin Verses
4th 12·30 – 1·30	Latin Prose	Latin Prose	Drawing	Latin Prose	Latin Prose	Drawing
5th 4·0 — 5·0	Latin Comp	Latin Comp	—	Latin Comp	Latin Comp	
6th 5·0 – 6·0	English	English		English	English	—
Prep. 7·30 — 8·30	Greek	French	Greek	French	French	Greek
Break 11·30 10·45 –			Music?	Drill	Gym	Music

A boy's timetable.

Though many old boys were critical of the Bear (Alington), GB, with his proneness to loyalty as well as hero-worship, became devoted to 'Uncle Hugh', as he called him:

> If I now look back on the Summer Fields of 1919, there is no doubt much to criticize. But I should like to make it clear that *then* I accepted everything

56

uncritically and that I was supremely happy – happy not only in being out of the army, but happy in my relationships with boys and masters. Moreover, I had a deep affection and respect for Uncle Hugh and realised how lucky I was to serve under him. If there were faults in the regime, I have condoned nearly all of them.

The rationale of Summer Fields under the Doctor had been the winning of scholarships, which at that time meant classical scholarships. The philosophy of the Maclarens had been *Mens Sana in Corpore Sano*; Archie Maclaren had trained the boys' bodies, while 'Mrs' had trained their minds. He had written books upon the value, indeed necessity, of physical education; she was a fine Greek scholar and became an inspiring teacher. Dr Williams was also an able teacher, but not so great a scholar. The veneration of games, especially cricket, came second to Classics, and the whole ethos was cemented by religion – as it would continue to be for many years to come. Not only the Doctor and the Bear were in holy orders, but also Cyril Williams, who took on the headmastership in 1928.

Discipline was strict; as at most such schools of that time, caning was part of everyday life. Classics and games dominated the timetable in and out of school hours. GB of course subscribed to both of these, but had his reservations:

> It was not so much that undue attention was paid to Latin and Greek; as a classical scholar *manqué* I approved of that. But over the many years of his rule Dr Williams (no scholar, but a great teacher) had regarded the defeat of the Eton examiners as the chief object of his life. Consequently he had evolved a system: in many ways it was a good system (his resounding triumphs at Eton and elsewhere bear witness to that), but it was far too rigid and doctrinaire and he would allow no deviations from it. If you pointed out that a word to which, in one of his rhymes, he gave a genitive plural in *-ium* had in fact *no* genitive plural, he would merely snort; but, if you questioned the extremely improbable rules that he had evolved for doing conditional clauses, you were almost in danger of the sack!

There is a story, repeated by both Strong and GB, that, when at a staff meeting some matter was under discussion and 'Bam' Evans started to demur, the Doctor turned on him and said, "If you do not like it, Evans, the remedy is in your own hands," and no more protesting was heard. Case did, however, stand up on occasion to the Doctor, who knew that he was too valuable and independent to risk such tactics. The fact that he was a martinet, however, should not detract from the Doctor's achievements, and did not diminish the respect and affection which most of his pupils felt for him. In the period from 1900 to 1919, Summerfieldians won 106 scholarships at Eton, including eight firsts, and 108 at other schools. The method worked, and those who were taught by it denied that it was 'cram' and maintained that it was exciting.

GB himself could see that the work that was good was supremely good.

> It wasn't the result of cram, as many envious Cascas alleged; blood and sweat there might be, toil and tears there certainly were; but the finished article was a

classical scholar superbly grounded by exceptional teachers. Nor was it only the scholars who benefited – another well-voiced slander. The ordinary pass boy was, in most cases, equally well grounded, admittedly in Latin and Greek alone, but that was all that the public schools asked for.

The Bear, who took on Fifth Form from the Doctor in 1917, carried on his system, and so did Smyth, though he was too good a scholar not to be aware of its defects; so did Cyril Williams, although he did not properly understand it. Willy-nilly, therefore, the other young men had to toe the line; but they could at least set about improving relations with boys out of school hours. There was an unwritten tradition that no master was ever about in the playing fields or in the boys' rooms unless he was on duty or taking part in some official game.

To us younger ones it seemed only natural to be about with the boys, playing chess or ping-pong with them, bowling to them or just talking to them. The older masters – except Case – looked askance at this innovation, and Crofts missed no opportunity of saying unpleasant things to the air in the hearing of the boys.

GB overlapped with Crofts by only a year, but it was sufficient for him to overcome his initial fear and develop respect and yes, even a little fondness. John Crofts had originally come to Summer Fields as a stopgap for a fortnight. That was in 1882, and he stayed till Christmas 1920. Born in 1854, he was not so very old when he retired, but he was long and thin and he had a pronounced stoop and a patriarchal beard.

J. F. Crofts.

To us and the boys he seemed a very Methuselah. I sat next to him at dinner on my first night and was almost petrified with fear. At heart he was a kindly man, but the necessity (in his view) of keeping the boys tightly reined in and his unsleeping vigilance in the interests of discipline had soured his temper. Until one got to know him, he really was rather awe-inspiring.

The boys called him Crab – his gait had something crablike about it – and a 'Crab bait', a thing of frequent occurrence, fairly made the rafters ring. Sometimes he would direct one, via the boys, at the young masters ('Crofts' Black Book', we used to call that). "Get off those pipes!" he would roar as he came into New Room and found JFE sitting on the hot-water pipes with half-a-dozen boys on either side of him. Once, in giving a boy a new exercise-book, I wrote his nickname instead of his surname on the cover; Crofts, to whom all slang and abbreviations were as abhorrent as they were to Penny (but we cured Penny), exploded with wrath when he found the book lying about – taking care to find it when I was in the room!

I remember the evening when Crofts was presented with a claret-jug by the boys after his retirement had been announced. JFE and I were so ill-bred as to listen at the door of New Room. Crofts' voice nearly broke with emotion as he tried to thank the boys; five minutes later he was in full cry down the passage in blaring pursuit of some wretched boy caught out of his room.

GB plunged happily into teaching; without qualification other than a university degree, as was the norm in those days, he soon found that he had discovered his métier. He taught Lower Shell at first – a middle-school form containing what he called in Wodehousian phrase some 'tough eggs'.

> They had enjoyed themselves at the expense of temporary war-time masters and they proposed to go on enjoying themselves at mine. Two of them, perhaps, were keen to learn; the others resisted strenuously. The strife was fierce for some weeks, but the weapons at the disposal of a master determined to enforce discipline are too powerful; he may get himself heartily disliked for a time (I did), but that is a small price to pay for peace in the form-room.

Later he was promoted to taking Lower Remove, which consisted of boys who would enter Fifth Form, the scholarship form, the next year. As well as teaching Classics, he also taught French, maths, English, history, geography and scripture. Space was at a premium, and for his maths lessons he had to share a room called Lower School with Crofts, who groaned audibly if GB raised his voice. At the beginning of the next term, however, he was shifted to Middle School, where he spent six happy years with Penny.

> I didn't enjoy teaching maths, but I did enjoy listening to Penny and ragging him without arousing the boys' suspicions.

This sharing of schoolrooms was common in many schools, and continued at Summer Fields until well into the 1950s.

Though living in Front Lodge, from 1924 onwards he had charge of seeing the boys in Cubicles to bed. Summer Fields occupied a number of buildings, and those where the boys slept were called lodges. These were not the equivalent of public-school 'houses', because one progressed through a number of different lodges during one's five years. The new boy started in the main building, called simply House, where he would probably spend two years, then proceed to Manor, Old Lodge or Cubicles, and spend his last year or two in Cottage or Mayfield. Just to confuse matters, Front Lodge was not a lodge in the sense of accommodation for boys, but merely a masters' colony, where GB lived happily for twenty years.

Cubicles was in a building attached by a corridor to the main house. It was built in the 1880s to house on three floors the school's kitchen, dining room and sleeping quarters for the domestics. This was adapted when in 1903 the Doctor built a large dining hall at the north end of the school; the vacated middle floor of the 1880 building was divided into 'loose-boxes' similar to those in Eton's Long Chamber, and some twenty boys slept there.

It was an unusual situation to have a master living elsewhere in charge of a lodge, and one that would not pass muster today. Presumably there were some adults in the building as the 'maids' slept on the floor above, and Miss Peirce, the formidable matron, also had some jurisdiction there. GB and she did not always see eye to eye.

> I cannot say that she was a lovable character, but she was incredibly efficient. She believed that boys (and young masters) should be brought up the hard way and she, who never spared herself, was not given to sparing others. At times her iron discipline overreached itself. A notice in the changing-room read, 'Any boy leaving his clothes about will hang them up twenty times under supervision'. I don't suppose that even Crofts bothered about that one. Another notice I found in Cubicles when I took over there: 'No boy to leave his bed before being called in the morning for any reason whatever'. Well, well.

Cubicles

The Vinery

1890 view of the school, showing Cubicles and the Vinery.

GB in fact modified this verbally to "for any reason except one". He was himself, however, reputedly very harsh to those who needed to go to the Vinery (Summer Fields name for the lavatory) during lessons.

The Vinery formed the topic of one of GB's favourite rebukes for the sloppy use of English – which was surely shared by many schoolmasters of the period.

"Please, sir, can I go to the Vinery?"

"I don't know whether you *can*, but you may."

However stern the discipline and inflexible the regime, there was time for fun. The war was over and, to their amazement, the young masters had survived it; what generation can have had a better excuse for ebullient, sometimes even childish, high spirits? As well as John Evans, GB found Bryan Buckley and Leonard Strong congenial, and he worshipped Billy Case; but he was also able to appreciate the older generation, and in particular F. P. Penny.

As Strong remarked, Penny could easily have been mistaken for the typical, dry-as-dust Victorian usher; that was how he appeared at first to any who heard him teach or saw him marching down the corridor, one hand grasping the *Morning Post*, the other thrust out in front of him as a protection against boys charging round the corner. But a kinder, more generous man can never have existed; he never forgot a kindness done to himself, and he cannot have remembered one half of those which he did to others. He was an efficient teacher, but scarcely an enlivening one. His methods, like his jokes, were cut and dried. The boys could often tell what his next words would be; those who committed the solecism in translation of writing, 'Caesar, which . . . ' invariably elicited the witticism, "Caesar wasn't a witch."

Case could give a superb imitation of him, but it was GB who inadvertently discovered his possibilities.

> One day in my second term, without realising that I was transgressing the code, I referred to a very dark morning as 'pitchers'. It didn't seem odd to me, but to Penny it appeared the quintessence of *argot*. He relayed it to Crofts, who grunted his disapproval, he bellowed it into Aunt Margaret's ear-trumpet, and punctually next morning he said to me, 'I suppose this is what *you* would call *pitchers*?' After that he had no chance; his education in slang proceeded apace and (after a few gasps of astonishment that people could really talk like that) he thoroughly enjoyed it.

The new young men obviously made a difference to the games coaching as well as to the general atmosphere of the school. When GB arrived, there was no rugby, but John Evans introduced it in the following year; Case took the cricket, and Smyth the soccer. The Bear also turned out three or four times a week on the soccer pitch, doing little coaching but taking an active part at the age of sixty-two. He adored soccer, having been in the Oxford side for two years, and he would berate the boys when they did the wrong thing. They were understandably nervous of him, but some good teams emerged. The school, however, showed a deplorable attitude to their teams in matches. This GB and Buckley set out to change.

> If it was a 1st XI match, the 2nd XI linked arms and barracked from the touch-line; 1st XI behaved similarly at a 2nd XI match. Why this was tolerated, I could never discover. Bryan Buckley and I were so horrified that we started organizing small cheer-groups. The boys were willing enough, but they had feared to break tradition.

Tradition was indeed strong under the reign of the Bear. Sunday in 1920 was probably very similar to a Sunday in 1870. Breakfast at 8.15 was followed by Bible-reading and letter-writing; choir-practice, and then chapel at eleven o'clock. After that came congregational practice at twelve and lunch at one. From two to three there would be a walk, and then two hours of sitting at desks until tea at five. An hour's scripture prep at 5.45 and chapel at seven rounded off the day. GB described it as 'truly a day of penance', but the boys liked it 'because it was different from other days'. Its structure and strictness were due to the Bear's own upbringing: one of a large family, he had grown up in a strict Victorian parsonage; what had been right for him as a child must be right for others. When some of the staff suggested that the afternoon might be more tolerable if boys were allowed, say, to bowl in the nets, the Bear was deeply hurt and dismissed the suggestion out of hand. On one wet Sunday, GB asked if he might play his gramophone to the boys. Permission was granted, but with the injunction, "Don't make it too secular." It would be interesting to know whether GB had any records of hymns, but most probably he hoped that Sullivan, as the composer of 'The Lost Chord' and 'Onward, Christian Soldiers', would pass muster.

Mumps appeared in the middle of the Lent term 1921 and, in order to get clear of it, term was extended by a fortnight. Those were the days of closely guarded quarantine periods and stern notes from schools to parents forbidding them to take their sons to 'public places of entertainment' or anywhere where they might pick up an infection during the last fortnight of the holidays. Not only was term extended but summer came early in March, and so for the last weeks of term there was no chance of playing soccer or rugger (of which the Bear did not really approve, but John Evans had somehow persuaded him to sanction it). GB noted that:

> Tom Hayward, wiser than we, put up the nets in the Parks. But our authorities would not do that; instead they condemned us to perpetual afternoons of golf. All very jolly for the golf-lover, but a pain in the neck for those allergic to the game, of whom I confess to being one. I have not often been bored at Summer Fields, but in the spring of 1921 I came perilously near to that condition.
>
> However, much as I disliked the game, I went on playing golf of a sort until March 1939. Then, in the Staff v Oxford OSS game, played on a bitterly cold day, I partnered John Evans and chose to think that he mucked up all my good shots – no doubt he was thinking the same of me. [They were beaten by Jimmy Bell, who would one day succeed GB with Fifth Form, and Nico Henderson, who subsequently joined the Foreign Office and rose to be our ambassador in Washington.] At the day's end I said, 'Nobody is going to make me play this what-not of a game again. After tea I am going to auction my clubs for the benefit of the Library.' And I did; but the boys bid so fantastically high for the clubs that they got them for nothing; all but my aluminium putter. That I kept *in piam memoriam*. But when the cry went up in the 1940s for aluminium to make Spitfires, I had to sacrifice it: I have always been sure that it did its stuff in the air as it had done on the ground.

As well as his academic teaching, GB helped with the soccer and the cricket, and was soon in charge of the Under-10 cricket team, which played its first match against Cothill in July 1922.

> Next year, unasked, I appointed myself coach of the Under-10 side and ran it for about 15 years, in addition to regular bowling at first-game nets. I enjoyed it tremendously, but found it more tiring than almost any other job. So I gave it up, but had to take it on again during the war and, with one year's intermission, continued to look after the Colts, as they were now called, until the end of the 1955 season.

Jimmy Bell and 'Puss' Henderson in the 1932 cricket XI. Below them are the captain, David Kay, and 'Bob' Purchas, who both later had sons at Summer Fields, and Harold Hartley, who, like JLB, returned to Summer Fields after the war as a master.

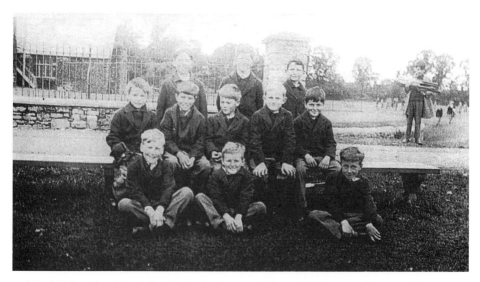

The 1922 under-10 cricket XI, its back row sadly vanishing into the mist: they are (standing) G. D. Rhys-Williams, C. Cunningham, T. R. Miles; (seated) F. B. Hartshorne, R. Thicknesse, D. L. L. Stewart (captain), P. H. Shaw-Stewart and H. J. Shaw; (on the ground) R. A. Roberts, C. E. Hartley and D. P. Macnee.

The concept of a Colts team in those days was under-10 rather than under-11, as it is now.

The year 1922 was in fact a sad one for Summer Fields cricket, for in March Billy Case, who had long had to be careful of his heart, died quite suddenly. His colleagues were desolated, and none more than GB, who said that:

> we who survive him know well that if we have been any good as schoolmasters our debt to him is incalculable. We younger ones could never have enough of him. He saw everybody's point of view and he had an extraordinary understanding of the way other people's thoughts were working. Small wonder that he was greatly loved by the boys and that his influence with us young masters was considerable.
>
> Often he made fun of his colleagues who had annoyed him. There was an occasion when someone with no great knowledge of cricket [presumably Cyril Williams from what comes next] had adversely criticized the batting of 1st XI in a match; Case was furious and, after expressing himself with some fervour, wound up with, 'What cricket club has he ever played for – except the Brasenose Improbables?' I had at that moment a mouthful of hot coffee; *had* is the operative word. [GB was a great giggler.]
>
> His manners were exquisite and his conversation polished. Even when he was reducing us to helpless laughter, he would often let fall (perhaps unconsciously) words of wisdom whose value to us was inestimable, though we probably didn't realise it at the time.
>
> He died very suddenly. On a Monday he was with us at coffee, obviously feeling unwell; by the Saturday he was dead from a clot of blood in the heart. As he was taken off to hospital [the Acland Nursing Home], he said to someone, 'I hope this isn't the end.' In one sense it was, but not, surely, in any sense that matters.

Case was succeeded by a Mr Davies, who lasted only one term. GB was on duty with 'this man', as he calls him, so:

> I had the full benefit of his strangeness. He was quite without shame or conscience, would turn up for his form if it suited him, but was far more likely to be in bed, 'sleeping it off', and never did a hand's turn of duty. We said good-bye to him without regret. He went to a Roman Catholic school where, as a heretic, he was never allowed to be on duty: it must have suited him well.

He was succeeded by A. F. ('Bobs') Alington, the youngest of the Bear's four sons, who took over French from Bam. French had not really been taken seriously in the upper forms, and Bobs had a tough job in bringing it up to standard. GB was promoted to take Division II. Smyth's departure a year or two later also resulted in promotion – to teach Classics to Lower Remove – the third form in the school. He was able to take up Greek again:

> I found I was pretty rusty in it, but the grounding of my second prep school stood me in good stead.

The climax of the academic year was, apart from the scholarships, the July exams. All the papers were of two hours' duration, and prize-giving lasted three hours. Speeches had to be made by the examiners in Classics (one covering the Upper School, another the Lower), maths and French. On one occasion Dr Williams talked for fifty minutes about the Upper School Classics; GB created something of a scandal when he got through in under half an hour!

In 1923, he asked if he might set the Upper School Classics exams, and found the excellence of Fifth Form a revelation, though, unsurprisingly, it was a Herculean task to mark all the papers – some sixty two-hour grammar papers to correct. It involved an all-night sitting.

> I don't know how I found time to compose a speech for prize-giving. That was an ordeal, too, with Doctor and Uncle Hugh sitting there; all their vast experience was, as it were, being subjected to the criticism of a tyro – much as if a village cricketer were to advise Ranjitsinhji on his execution of the leg glance. Not that I went as far as that, but I did venture one or two criticisms, and this brought out the best in Uncle Hugh. He said nothing at the time but, when I was saying good-bye next day, he went out of his way to compliment me on my report. That was entirely typical of him.

After the death of Case, John Evans had taken over the running of Cottage, and, as mentioned above, Bobs Alington joined the staff that autumn. The following April he married Gillian Tanner, and they went to live in a house in the Banbury Road. But Margaret Alington felt that her son, as one of the successors to the founders' inheritance, ought not to be living as it were in exile, but should be in charge of one of the boys' houses. Had she reflected, she would have realised that this would happen soon anyway when the Bear retired; but she did not reflect.

Without consulting her husband, she induced Gill to approach John Evans with the astounding suggestion that he and the other Cottage masters should go and live in the Banbury Road, while Bobs and Gill took over Cottage. GB takes up the tale:

> This was a colossal blunder, and the repercussions were endless. I got the full force of the storm, for it happened that I was going to Stowe with John on the day that the balloon went up [this was 1926]. He talked of nothing else on the drives there and back; indeed, he talked of nothing else for the rest of the term. In principle my sympathies were all with him and I did my very best to make Bobs and Gill see that the suggestion should never have been made. But jealous feelings had been aroused and many bitter things were said. Eventually Uncle Hugh got to hear of it and his comment was characteristic: 'Who started all this rot anyway?' Of course he vetoed the move, but John handed the rugger over to Bobs and, a year later, the cricket also. I did my best to stop this last, but John was ever one to cut off his nose to spite his face!
>
> Naturally, the row died down in time, and Bobs and Gill had only a year to wait before they moved to Mayfield, which suited them much better than Cottage would have done. But Bobs and John never really saw eye to eye again; seeds of mistrust had been sown and the harvest was inevitable. I don't think it an exaggeration to say that this incident changed the course of the School's history.

CHAPTER 4: LIFE AND LITERATURE

DURING THE 1920s several younger men joined the permanent staff: Ralph Robinson, Bobs Alington, Roger Jacques, Geoffrey Frodsham, Llewellyn Jeffreys-Jones and Hubert Mullins. The school was still largely a bachelor establishment, and some of these were indeed confirmed bachelors. Such a phrase, used post-war, might mean at least a misogynist and at most a homosexual or, more specifically, a pederast. In his excellent study of *The English Boys' Boarding Preparatory School 1918–1940*, Jonathan Austin examines this issue perceptively:

> The fact that most [schoolmasters] were bachelors leads late twentieth-century readers to make conclusions that may be wide of the mark . . . The automatic assumption is made that they preferred the company of men and were therefore homosexual. This is not only unfair but incorrect . . . There were more significant reasons why masters stayed single.
>
> Primary among these was the fact that traditionally it had been an all-bachelor occupation. At all-male institutions a masculine atmosphere was deeply pervading . . . The longer masters lived in such an environment, the more inhibited and idiosyncratic they became, the very idea of living with a woman becoming an impossibility.

This last sentence may be something of an overstatement, for Penny, who got married in late middle age, shows that there were exceptions. But the general principle that it was a society which did not easily accommodate wives holds good; and in certain ways bachelorhood was desirable for the long hours that assistant masters were expected to work. As we have seen, masters like GB and John Evans wanted to spend spare time with the boys and knew it to be a good thing to do so.

There is a danger of reading too much into a situation. The period between the wars was one of comparative innocence and ignorance, and it may be difficult for us, who have sex thrust at us non-stop by screaming media, to enter the pre-war point of view. GB had grown up in a number of male-dominated institutions: school, university, the army, and now here he was at school again. He certainly respected many women and was on good terms with them, including mothers of Summer Fields boys. Equally, there is no doubt that he felt deep affection for several of his pupils, and was never happier than when in their company: they may have been substitutes for the sons that he never had or they may have been the objects of deeper, sublimated desires; but to say more than that would be to jump to conclusions on inadequate evidence. He did have favourites, but perhaps the very frankness with which he favoured them shows how innocent he at least considered his favouritism to be. The years 1931–5 in his photograph album contain some forty pictures in which one particular boy is the main or only subject.

GB's taste in literature both dictated and revealed his attitude to women and, indeed, men. If one believes that he identified with Psmith, Jeeves, Sherlock Holmes, Raffles and even Ukridge, one may feel that in his book the ideal companion was another man. Psmith had Mike (who was designed to be the central character of a fairly traditional, but superior, school story until Psmith's originality put him delicately into second place); Jeeves had Wooster, Holmes had Watson, Raffles had Bunny and Ukridge had Corky.

In most of these pairs, the companion played the second fiddle, and Boswell to the protagonist's Johnson. The relationship is comfortable, affectionately teasing, rarely emotional. Emotion and sex, such as it is, find other outlets. Mike marries Phyllis (but she does not feature much in the Psmith stories). Bertie pursues various unsuitable, usually domineering, young women, until he is rescued by Jeeves and restored to the straight-and-narrow bachelor life of the Berkeley Mansions flat and the Drones Club. Holmes has little time for women – his regard for the superior mental attributes of Irene Adler was a notable exception – and Watson marries (possibly twice), but drops his wife, as well as his medical practice, with alacrity if Holmes wants him for a case. Ukridge is totally self-absorbed. Bunny is the most emotional of these characters, and he hero-worships Raffles in between rather pettish moods.

Raffles was certainly a cricket hero – 'a dangerous bat, a brilliant field and perhaps the very finest slow bowler of his decade' – but he tended to speak slightingly of the game. This would be blasphemy to GB, who did, however, allow himself to disparage various other ball games, such as golf and tennis, which he invariably called 'patters' (i.e. patball). Raffles is also the most amoral of these fictional heroes, but each of the others is prepared to bend at least the law, if not the moral code. Holmes is an efficient housebreaker. Jeeves knocks out an inconvenient adversary, observing that one cannot make an omelette without breaking eggs. Psmith works a deliberate course of deceit upon the pompous Mr Downing (he probably owes not a little to Kipling's Stalky in his original characterisation). Ukridge deceives everybody; he is the Lord of Misrule – a point we shall discuss further.

Did GB have an 'ideal companion'? Probably only in literature. In life, John Evans, who in a sense he partnered for twenty-five years, complemented him in many ways, but they did not invariably get on well. Geoffrey Alington might have become Psmith to his Mike. He was not the only companion that the war deprived GB of; there was his brother Billy, who died in the Dardanelles when barely twenty. He may well have been closest to GB in sympathy as well as age, and almost certainly something of GB died in the war that killed so many of his friends.

He was an emotional man, but he kept a rein upon most of his emotions. The

2.

3.

5.

4.

Characters from GB's album, 1931–3
1. & 3. Henry Shaw, whom GB nicknamed 'Captain'
Shaw, as in the Fairy Queen's song in Iolanthe.
2. shows Henry, GB and Tim Barclay evidently having
a 'bad cricket day'.
4. & 5. show GB with the Shaw-Stewart brothers,
Patrick and Michael; GB often stayed with their family
in Morar during the holidays.

6.

7.

8.

9.

6., 7. & 8. The annual Hay Feast was one of Summer Fields' best and most enjoyed traditions, in which each form built, and then defended, a hay hut. John Poole, John Hext, the Close twins and Christopher Lee are gathering hay, but not as wholeheartedly as Jimmy Bell (7.), and Pat Shaw-Stewart and Frank Hartshorne (8.) are taking their ease. Patrick Macnee was known as Smee (9.), after the pirate in Peter Pan. He was quite a mischievous boy and a fine actor, as subsequent events confirmed.

one that he did allow himself to indulge was anger. This was a safety valve, a release – though the boy-recipients of his wrath would not have seen it in quite that light! Another safety valve was literature; here one was allowed to display emotion and even go against the mores of society, which was still full of repression though the war had started to break down barriers and dilute inhibitions.

Once, when asked which character in the Savoy Operas he would most have liked to play, he named Jack Point. This was not a spur-of-the-moment reply. Jack Point is the jester who collapses unconscious or possibly dies of a broken heart at the end of *The Yeomen of the Guard*. He has pathos, but also, by the nature of his profession, is allowed licence in his behaviour and the way he looks at things. Here we come to the Lord of Misrule, and the attractiveness of disorder, even crime, to one who led an orderly and 'proper' life.

Henry Lytton as Jack Point in The Yeomen of the Guard, *from* The Sphere.

Two literary characters which might suggest GB are Mr Chips and Andrew Crocker-Harris. Most good schools have, or have had, a Mr Chips and are the better for it – somebody who gives continuity over a long period by total identification with the establishment, indeed love of the institution and all it stands for. This was not hard for GB: very early, Summer Fields became his second home, and he evidently looked upon 'Uncle Hugh' and 'Aunt Margaret' as his second family, even though his own parents both lived to a great age (Chloe died in 1944; and Henry, 1948). In due course the school became his first home, and surely occupied first place in his heart – above even the Parks and Hove.

Andrew Crocker-Harris, 'the Himmler of the Lower Fifth' in Terence Rattigan's play,
The Browning Version.

Crocker-Harris in Terence Rattigan's play *The Browning Version* appears at first sight to be a dried-up, petty tyrant whose youthful enthusiasms have turned sour. And so, to some extent, he is; but the power of the play lies in his being forced into a position where he shows emotion and becomes indeed a type of martyr figure. GB led too happy a life for this cap to fit, but there may have been a touch of Crocker-Harris in some of his form-room dealings with boys: the uneasy aura of fear, the whispered words of rebellion at the back of the room. But anger was not a weapon used by the 'Himmler of the Lower Fifth': he would not permit himself that outlet. And, outside school hours, his only contact with the boys would be extra Classics.

GB, as we know, adored free time and being with the boys. Many, though not all, responded to his approaches. We have heard about the 'funny jokes in Greek before breakfast'; and Julian Amery's attitude to GB (see the next chapter, page 88) probably represented at least a minority of his contemporaries. But then this boy and the master would have had such radically different ideas as to how to spend spare time that there could be little common ground. GB was happy reading to boys, giving them fielding practice or kicking a football about with them, playing chess or ping-pong (never to be called table tennis!) or, best of all, taking them to watch cricket, though this was commoner with old boys or other adult friends.

John Evans and GB did purvey a sort of 1920s atmosphere. Their rooms smelt of Turkish tobacco or possibly Sullivans, as smoked by Raffles. ("Have a gasper – Turkish this side, Virginia that.") The furniture was Victorian, and books, even more than ashtrays, formed a major feature of the ensemble – as did framed photographs on desk- or table-tops. GB had photographs of Patrick Macnee and Robin Sinclair in the 1935 production of *Richard II*, together with several others, one of which was possibly his brother Billy. The wind-up gramophone and record cabinet full of the Savoy Operas lent a more up-to-date period touch.

Obviously his huge collection of Wodehouse and the complete Wisden dominated his bookshelves. The former were largely wrapperless, most of them being faded orange and featuring the Herbert Jenkins colophon; the latter were a discreet and distinguished brown, also faded with gold lettering, though the collection included some of the yellow softback editions. What else would there be? Kipling of course; Bernard Shaw and H. G. Wells (Mr Polly is quoted in the preface to the *History of the O.U.C.C.*); some elderly editions of classical authors and some notebooks of his own, including the soccer books in which he wrote up every match while he was in charge of the soccer. JFE and Bobs did the same for the rugger. After the write-up, these books were circulated for the team to read; when they were filled up, they were added to the school library – which was also under GB's care.

The first soccer book begins with the match against Magdalen College School on 20th October 1926:

Lost 6–0. Well played! It was a good show, whatever the score may look like; and we don't usually reckon to beat an older and heavier side. But 3–1 against us would have been quite a reasonable result to this game. Full marks to everyone for <u>guts</u> and <u>go</u> – & those are what really count. If you keep up today's effort you ought to be a jolly good side when you've got the necessary experience.

This is generous in defeat and sensible, in that it shows faith in the team and will surely encourage them to greater efforts. Not all the match accounts were kindly, however; the other GB appears only too soon in the write-up of the next game:

> 2nd XI v Cothill 1st XI, Oct 23. Won 2–1. We don't generally reckon to beat Cothill with our 2nd XI, so thus far it was a very good show. The trouble is that with a little more vim and guts we should have reached double figures. This does not apply to the halves, all of whom played splendidly; so did the full-backs, and the wings were very decent. BUT the three insides – it's no good disguising the fact – were simply deplorable. Hunter in the first half and Barclay in the second made <u>some</u> attempt to do the right thing, though they usually ended by muddling their wing or their half. Of Trevaskis the less said the better. I have never seen a more gutless display of incompetence and he must buck up and put his back into it if he is to improve.

Trevaskis survived this demolition to soar to great heights in the Foreign Office as Sir Kennedy Trevaskis, high commissioner in Aden and a governor of Summer Fields; so perhaps GB's excoriation did bring out some vim and guts in him!

Reviews of the matches each season appeared in the school magazines, of which GB was also editor from 1930 to 1946, and here he was generous in his praise and more circumspect in censure. He was also particularly laudatory about the school plays. Time and again he says in effect, 'We couldn't imagine a better production than last year's, but this one was even better.' He was in no doubt about Patrick Macnee's gifts. In 1934 he writes:

> Henry V cannot be written down a great play. Undeniably, however, it has its moments, and these were fully brought out in this production . . . I find it a little difficult to write of Macnee's Henry. I don't want to use the language of exaggeration or to suggest that Macnee is a second Irving; but when I consider that in less than a month he had to learn some seven or eight hundred lines and that he was to all intents and purposes word-perfect in them I find it hard to restrain my admiration. That, too, without considering his acting at all. . . . I venture to say that his delivery of his two great speeches was wellnigh perfect. He was also excellent in the rather tiresome and uncongenial Glove scenes and in the final scene with the Princess. And that is all I am going to write of Macnee, lest I should be tempted to write too much. But I could not readily forget the beautiful effect of the slow curtain on 'O God of battles'.

Next year, it was *Richard II*. The review was by Nevill Coghill, but GB sets the scene:

> There was a space of just over three weeks between the first rehearsal and the final production. Lest any should cry, 'Summer Fields cramming again', let me add that the time usually available for rehearsal was about two hours a day. I do not think that any other words are necessary to pay tribute to the producers and to the boys themselves, notably to Sinclair and Macnee . . .

Ten years later, at the end of the war and in a paper shortage, another *Richard II* receives this tribute:

> To some of us it seemed a daring move to put on *Richard II*, and the *laudator temporis acti* shook a head as heavy as the eldest oyster's. He need not have worried. One cannot compare the performance with that of 1935, the inconveniences of having to play in the dining-room instead of the gym alone precluding comparison; and it is probably true to say that there is not so much natural acting talent in the top part of the school as there was ten years ago. With those slight reservations one can offer the heartiest congratulations to producers and cast.

GB also wrote generously in praise of colleagues, and over the years, not only of his editorship, he penned some moving tributes, notably to Billy Case (see page 64), and Margaret Alington, who died in 1938.

> From the time when I first met her in 1915; through the war years when, with all the cares of the School upon her, she yet found time to write regularly and at length to friends at the front; and throughout the eight years that I worked under her and Uncle Hugh (I cannot possibly use the terms Mr and Mrs Alington), her entire and absolute devotion to Summer Fields and all that it stood for was what struck one most forcibly. It is not unusual to speak of a person as unselfish: Aunt Margaret was selfless. An old servant of the school once said to me, 'You know, sir, Mrs Alington does consider you masters'; this was perfectly true – she 'considered' every one. I have heard her quote her mother's dictum: 'Boys first, masters second, family last'; had she added 'self nowhere' she would have but put into words the principle of her daily life.

Generous in praise, GB was also generous with his possessions. Over the years, many of his books found their way from his shelves to those of the school library or to pupils and ex-pupils; the present author, for instance, received a set of Thucydides and one of Herodotus as well as a large Liddell and Scott Greek Lexicon. His encyclopaedic knowledge and love of literature were things that GB delighted in handing down to the boys.

School photo, 1928.

CHAPTER 5: FIFTH FORM

'BEAR' ALINGTON had a stroke in October 1927, and his doctor told him that he must retire; he is reputed to have thought for a minute on receiving this ultimatum, and then said, "Thank heavens I shall never beat a boy again!" His retirement meant that Cyril Williams now became headmaster with Bobs Alington as his partner. But would Cyril also take on Fifth Form? It was in the Summer Fields tradition to expect that he would, but there were two reasons for his not doing so, immediately at any rate. He had been about to go away for an operation, and he had doubts about his own ability as a Classics teacher at that level.

Cyril saw no reason to postpone his operation. GB feared that chaos might result.

> This meant that an untried Bobs was in command, a Bobs who was violently anti the old régime (notably the Classics) and who, the wish being father to the thought, felt sure that Cyril would never come back. John [Evans] and I had been on the point of seeking our fortunes elsewhere, but clearly we could not go yet. To John fell the task of restraining Bobs, of making him see that he was not yet in command and of insisting that no major change be made until we knew what was going to happen. By so doing he undoubtedly saved Bobs from a row with the Doctor which could have had but one termination.

It is interesting that Bobs apparently believed that Cyril would not return from what was allegedly a minor nasal operation; also that John and GB already seem to be acting as partners. Both put loyalty to the school before their personal ambitions, and both were soon rewarded. After a certain amount of debate, GB was offered Fifth Form until Cyril's return, when the situation would be reviewed.

> I remember being walked round the field by the Doctor and being given some sort of briefing, always with the strong implication that I was only a stand-in. I didn't mind that. I was in a state of azure funk at the prospect, but I was also considerably excited by it and elated at having been chosen for what was unquestionably a post of honour.

After three weeks, Cyril came back and summoned GB to hear the plan that he had evolved. Basically, it was that they should share Fifth Form, GB taking them for composition, Cyril for translation. It would never have worked, and GB quite rightly refused to entertain the idea.

I was no obstructionist: I was perfectly willing to hand over to Cyril, for it was his birthright and I did not feel that I had any claims at all. I suppose I hoped that he wouldn't take it, but I was quite sincere and should have felt no sort of grievance if he had done so.

Possibly with some relief, Cyril decided not to, and GB was given Fifth Form on a year's probation.

I had one reminder that I was not above human failings. While taking Lower Remove, I had also been taking a Maths form and two French ones. Despite my prayers – for I have always loathed Maths – I had to keep the Maths (only for a term, as it turned out) and was taken off the French. When I told my senior French form that I was leaving them, they made all the proper noises of regret; but at the other end of the Gym was working my other French form and, when I told them, they gave three rousing cheers. A little humbling does one no harm. So began the most interesting and responsible job I had yet had to tackle.

His elation at getting it was matched by an apprehension that he might fail at it. With Lower Remove he had been able to recapture the groundwork of the classics, but he had not written a Latin prose or read a Greek play since before the war, and he had no knowledge of the dreaded *Borva Notes* (see page 112). Nor had he seen *Anglice Reddenda* since his own schooldays – this was a selection of Latin and Greek passages made in 1879 by C. S. Jerram of Woodcote House and, incidentally, it was still in Fifth Form use in the 1980s. In order to keep one jump ahead of Fifth Form, he had to use every minute of his spare time; he reckoned he put in eight hours' preparation most Sundays.

It paid off, and once again his luck was in. Four of the ten boys in Fifth Form had already had a year with the Bear, and 'really knew their stuff'. Well they might, when one considers that out of a total of thirty-eight hour-long lessons per week, Classics had twenty-three: one on Wednesdays, two on Saturdays, four on Mondays, five each on Tuesdays and Fridays, and six on Thursdays! Of the fifteen remaining lessons, maths got eight, leaving seven for the other subjects, including English. The justification for this was that in the Eton scholarships only Classics really counted, in that the final order was produced by the masters who set the Classics papers. This system obtained until 1942.

There are times when, however little we deserve it, everything comes off for us. We had an unexpected success at Harrow in the Easter term and then won first scholarship at Bradfield early in May. So we went to Eton, five from Fifth Form and two from Upper Remove, in good heart. The boys were in terrific spirits, and I had to pretend to be!

I had had a little experience in taking boys up for scholarships at Harrow and Charterhouse. But this was very different: it was, so to say, Test Match cricket, and I was making my debut in it. My acquaintance with Eton was slight, I knew hardly any of the masters, and I was scared stiff, though I did my best to conceal the fact.

H. K. Marsden. (Eton photographic archive)

School Yard, Eton College.
Long Chamber is behind the first-storey windows on the left of the picture.

In those gracious days all candidates were invited to luncheon in College Hall. By no means everybody accepted, but we always did. In 1928 the Master-in-College was none other than H. K. Marsden, reputed to be a fierce hater of Summer Fields and all its works. I sat down with our boys as far below the salt as I could get; but on the second day HKM swooped down on me with a characteristic "Come away from those women (two parents of candidates) and talk to me." So began a long acquaintance with this remarkable man. He was nearing the end of his time in College, but he had many more years to go at Eton and is popularly believed to have been one of the best house-masters ever. I find no difficulty in subscribing to this belief, but at that time he was just Bloody Bill, who hated Summer Fields – or so men said.

Somehow we got through that Tuesday and Wednesday, and then the final agony began. In those days a list was put up of the boys who had 'got into the Viva'; those who hadn't were not required to do the last paper. Hearing that the list would probably be up on Wednesday evening, I went down to Eton twice that night and once before breakfast on Thursday, all to no purpose. So I said that we must all go down to the Verses exam and hope for the best. Hardly had we started than we met several Old Boys running up the hill to tell us that we were all in. First staggering relief!

When we got back to Oxford, I thought that we'd better go to the Parks and watch the cricket for a bit – I didn't feel that I could face the School yet! But the boys were now in a state of high excitement and were beginning to behave badly, so I started them home. I saw Cyril on the other side of the road, obviously looking for us. The telegram had come from Eton [in the latter years of the century one had to wait three or four days] and we learnt that Fifth Form had achieved 1st, 2nd, 3rd, 5th and 10th, and Upper Remove 17th and 21st. And that was that. For the rest of the term we read Homer and did not overwork ourselves.

Julian Amery, as he appears in his photograph album: 'Let me introduce myself.'

The next few years were not so successful, and GB admitted that his own inexperience might have been a contributory factor. But there was also bad luck – a combination of circumstances militating against him. In 1928, two Summerfieldians had failed the Common Entrance, in spite of scoring over 70% in Latin. The anti-Classics brigade, led by Bobs and possibly with some support from Strong, saw their opportunity and pounced. There was a cut in the time given to Classics, a reduction from twenty-three hour periods to twenty forty-minute ones (in effect just over thirteen hours). In 1930, the best candidate, who would surely have got an Eton award, opted for Charterhouse; of those who tried for Eton, one was ill and another just returned from his sickbed.

> The only other candidates fit in body were by no means fit in mind. So for the first time in over sixty years, the Eton list contained no Summer Fields name.

This did not happen again under GB's aegis, nor under that of his successor, Jimmy Bell; but the present author, who succeeded him, had some blank years at Eton.

> The 1931 form were frankly a poor lot, but there were some young boys in it who needed only experience. Consequently 1932 was a very good year – five names on the Eton list and 100% elsewhere – and for the next twenty years, with some lapses (the 1933 form was the worst ever!) we kept up a pretty reasonable standard.

In all, during GB's twenty-five years at this particular helm, Summer Fields won eighty-two scholarships at Eton and fifty-six elsewhere; these others including Bradfield, Charterhouse, Clifton, Eastbourne, Felsted, Harrow, Malvern, Marlborough, Radley, Repton, Sedbergh, Shrewsbury, St Edward's, Stowe, Tonbridge, Wellington, Westminster and Winchester.

GB was no respecter of persons, and he left the 1933 Fifth Form in no doubt that it was the worst ever, just as he ensured that David James, of the 1932 football side, was always remembered for having missed an open goal. There was a form in 1943–4 called Fifth Form B, according to Jonathan Balcon, "not really scholarship material, but there was a slight hope that . . . we might achieve something". GB always referred to these boys to their faces as 'bogi', presumably meaning that they had no real claim to be called Fifth Form. Similarly, years later, when he had given up Fifth Form and was taking Lower Fifth, he would read out the weekly order, ending with "and, as usual, bringing up the rear, Messrs Broke, Poole & Wilson Ltd – *very* limited."

There was a form (which later became two forms) at Summer Fields called the Modern Side; these were the boys who did not do Greek, and they tended to be looked down upon – not particularly inspiring for their self-confidence. Probably this treatment of them as anathema stemmed from the Doctor, who was apt to tell boys who weren't doing well that they were 'a thorn in his side'. Certainly when Bobs Alington departed in 1937 to become an Inspector of Schools, the Doctor referred to him in a letter as 'the youngest Alington with his modernside ideas and hatred of the Classics'.

Characteristically of his generation GB was an inveterate and interesting letter-writer. In April 1938, he laments to Brian Straton-Ferrier that:

> V form did rather ill on the Sham Schols – a good deal worse than I expected them to do. I knew that Ted Close wouldn't do any good in the Harrow exam . . . but I have been hoping for fair results at Eton this year (Paget, Ted Guinness and Angus) & now I'm not so sure! Fawcus <u>ought</u> to do something at Stowe, but he's such a head-loser that he is quite capable of being ploughed on the prelim. Drew is going in for Winchester as a dark horse, but on his Sham Schols he was painfully dark. Remains one Godfrey Freeman who is to try for S. Edward's. His vaulting ambition thinks in terms of Radley and Marlborough, undeterred by the fact that, if he got top scholarship at either, he couldn't possibly afford to be there, but as he has hitherto omitted the formality of doing any work (24% on his Greek prepositions, je vous demande) his Classics must be considered rocky. However, I think we have at last got each other taped, & as he's by no means a fool, he might yet do something.
>
> Not very much other news. H.M.M. is being married on 20th, but most of us will be abroad at that time. I'm off to the Avignon district next week. I had meant to go to Rome, but with the situation so delicate in Central Europe I had visions of being caught out there when the battle began & being interned for the duration!

GB seems to have absolutely no doubt that the war will come. As for his other forecasts, Paget got a scholarship at Eton, but was the only one to do so: Guinness reached the Viva, i.e. a near miss; this was also Fawcus's fate at Stowe; and Freeman was successful at St Edward's. Drew was successful at Eton in the following year.

GB's teaching methods were an adaptation of the Doctor's. There was a lot of learning by rote, and the assumption was that the best way Fifth-Formers could fill their spare time if not playing cricket was by learning their grammar or vocabulary. To assist them, GB evolved a number of mnemonics over the years, as well as publishing a number of books. His first was *Aids to French Composition*, which appeared in 1925, published by Lakeman & Co., and costing 4s. 6d. It was reviewed skittishly in the *Summer Fields Magazine* by an anonymous reviewer, possibly Cyril Williams, who was editor at the time.

> Here at last is a French book, which, while never shirking any issues, yet by its simplicity, clearness and vigour, 'gets across' its points in the shortest and most interesting way . . . The sentences are human. They appeal to boys. They are also the sort of sentences you might expect to use in France . . . Latin and Greek are used to illustrate rules – an excellent plan, both on account of derivations and schools' curriculums. One of the best and biggest parts of the book is its appendix where, in the space of a few pages, you may learn such widely different things as the French for an April shower, a decalitre, a 2nd-class carriage, a meatless meal, Palm Sunday, whitebait, a kingfisher, Czechoslovakia, and forget-me-nots.

GB's attitude to France, its people and the French language is hard to fathom. He frequently quoted French in his memoirs (*'femme souvent varie'*, when one might have expected a classicist to go for *'femina semper mutabilis'*); yet, after the war, he seldom crossed the Channel, and never to visit France.

Classical books followed: *A Greek Vocabulary* (1944), *A Greek Grammar* (1946), *Junior Latin Composition* (1946) and (1951). The vocabulary was a paperback; the other three all contained mnemonic verses – it is hard to tell at this stage of time which were simply inherited (from Kennedy, for instance, or from some earlier Summerfieldian source) and which were original. A rhyme about Latin verbs governing the dative case appears in the Composition book, but seems to be familiar to non-Summerfieldians. In all these verses, it must be borne in mind that, as with Kennedy's gender rhymes, the 'old' pronunciation of Latin as if it were English, will achieve the rhyme. Here is a longish one about gerundives:

> Now of Gerundives let us treat,
> Expressing 'ought' or 'must' or 'meet';
> (Do not let us swear or cuss)
> The usual ending is in -**dus**;
> Viz, **amandus et monendus**,
> **Audiendus et regendus**.
>
> If the verb is transitive,
> Gerundive is an adjective
> Agreeing with a noun; thus, 'She
> Is meet to be advised by me',
> All good boys at once will render
> **Ea mihi est monenda**.
> (Note the **agent**'s case or state: I've
> Had to put it in the **dative**.)

When the verb is neuter (see?),
'To Rome it must be come by me',
Thus it should be done (*agendum*)
Est mihi Romam veniendum.

If the verb a dative takes
('I must give the boy some cakes'),
Then the **agent**, let me say,
Goes in the **ablative with 'a'**:
'**A me puero placentae**
Dandae sunt;' if that's not plenty,
'**Tullio a te, Antoni,**
Parcendum fuit Ciceroni.'

Another in similarly colloquial vein is the declension of *plus*:

Now just attend to me, my dears,
and don't make any fuss;
but listen hard with all your ears
while **I** discourse on **plus**.
It's **plus** in Nom. and Voc. and Acc.,
as any child can see;
pluris in Gen., we Dative lack,
the Ablative's **plure**.
Plures and **plura** we go on,
then (help!) it's **plurium**;
and finally to **pluribus**
we naturally come.

Others were to avoid confusions: a quintet of nouns in **gen-**, and this one:

Cancer (ablative **cancro**)
tells of crabs that sideways go;
carcer (masculine) will be
prison-cell for you and me
if we don't put **carcere**;
some there are who much prefer
when on horse to use **a spur**:
calcar (neuter) let them try,
ablative is **calcari.**

These work well for pupils who have a particular sort of mind, but others might merely find them tiresome and onerous, judging that it is easier simply to learn:

cancer, abl. cancro, m: crab.
carcer, abl. carcere, m: prison.
calcar, abl. calcari, n: spur.

According to Ian Tamworth, GB devised a hexameter mnemonic for distinguishing between the Latin nouns *sanguis* (the general word for blood) and *cruor* (specifically spilt blood or gore):

Sanguis inest venis, cruor est de corpore fusus.

Shortly after this, I had to translate the moving episode in the Fall of Troy as described by Vergil when Priam appears 'per aras sanguine foedentem'. Very unwisely, I remarked that it was a pity that the bard had not enjoyed the benefit of a classical education at SF – which immediately earned me an entry into the Black Book on a charge of impertinence.

Another outcome of the Bear's retirement was that GB took on the soccer. He had already started refereeing home matches upon Smyth's departure in 1924.

In my last Easter term at Repton in 1912 I kicked a football away from me, saying, 'That's the last time in my life I'll touch a soccer ball.' I never was much good as a prophet, but here I excelled myself. I had liked soccer at my prep school, but I hated it at Repton and was quite determined never to play it again. At Summer Fields I played it for close on thirty seasons, during 21 of which I was in charge of it! I had not, I believe, thought much about the games side of schoolmastering, but I found that I was expected to play four afternoons a week on 1st, 2nd or 3rd game, and I enormously enjoyed doing so. The star footballer of all my time was Derek Lomax (SF 1915–21), who was afterwards in the Oxford side for four years. He was a wonderful centre-half of the attacking variety and in his year as captain we beat Horris Hill twice – a feat that we have all too rarely achieved since.

GB had also taken on the magazine, when Cyril was promoted in 1928. This was something that he was to do for nineteen years, and in addition he acted as the school's archivist. Throughout the late 1920s he had been preparing a *School Register*, and it finally appeared in July 1929, a slim volume in Summerfieldian-red cloth with gold lettering, containing names and biographical details of the 1700-odd pupils who had passed through the school in its first sixty-five years. It also contained appendices with lists of the main teaching staff, scholars, football and cricket XIs and the roll of honour from the Great War.

The task of compiling a register of the School [the magazine informed its readers], which was begun before the war by the Rev. C. H. S. Gmelin, has been at last completed. Quite apart from the sheer labour of assembling the necessary details and seeing the manuscript through the press, the compiler's task was increased by the fact that, over long periods in the School's history, no adequate records had been kept. Advertisements were accordingly inserted in *The Times*, inviting all OSS to send particulars of their careers: a mountain of correspondence was faithfully levelled: and the compiler became also secretary and treasurer for the undertaking, soliciting, receiving and acknowledging the abundant flow of subscriptions.
    By this time anyone with the slightest knowledge of Summer Fields will have guessed the compiler's name . . . Mr Bolton.

Such compilations were a labour of love to GB, whose tidy mind enjoyed tabulating people, facts and even figures. An equal pleasure was the magazine, which he set about transforming in various ways. It was still predominantly composed of sports results and reviews and old-boy news, but in July 1928 he introduced an editorial and a spoof excerpt from Lucian about cricket; this included the appeal οὐσθάτ, and the schoolboy cries of χίζ and σνῦ, σνῦ ('snoo' being what in those days one said when verbally squashing an opponent).

In July 1929, he greeted the arrival of *The Universal*, a boy-edited magazine, which he later plundered (with permission) for material.

> We remember a very entertaining production in 1921, with very talented contributors; but, unlike the *Universal*, it circulated more or less privily in manuscript, and members of the staff saw it only by special courtesy. For this there was good reason, as they were therein lampooned with greater freedom than some of them would have appreciated.

This was the *Summer Fields Herald*, edited by John Lehmann and his fellow Fifth-Formers and brimming with subversive comments about the Bear, Case, Penny, Miss Peirce and others.

The
Summer Fields Herald
No. 1.   Over 5,000,000,000,000,00 sale.   Sunday. 1st October.

APPALLING WHISKEY SCANDAL!

DISGRACEFUL WHISKEY
SCANDAL REVEALED!!
Shall we stand this
drunkenness?
Last night, while the well-
known Mr Freese was
conducting the last sitting of
the Bown Notes Committee, a
certain member of the same
committee chanced to look
into the high cupboard which
contains the property of W.
S. Case Esq, the notorious
master (?). In it was discovered
two empty whiskey bottles,
evidently belonging to the aforesaid
W.S. Case Esq. No doubt the
fees will again be put up on
this account. Can patriotic
[cont. Page 2]

The Level Crossing
Question.
[By our special correspondent]
This Sunday again we
have been submitted the
indignity of a walk to the
level Crossing — the No man's
Land of Oxford. We look
around us now and see
many pleasant walks which
could be undertaken. For
the aeroplane enthusiast
Port meadow, or for others
Ham and Eggs, or the Park,
or Marston Ferry — anything
But the filthy and squalid
way which we have been
for two consecutive

Sundays. When a certain
F.P.P—Esq is on duty, we
can expect nothing else,
and we resign ourselves to
our untimely Fate. But
as today, when such a
master as J.E.E whom any
one can twist round their
little finger, is on duty,
we expect something more.
We must demand a redress
of this disgrace, & a
strike must be organised.
Readers are offered to
submit their opinions.
We have already been
crushed and been tyrannised!
But never
again must this happen!

The 1929 edition also contained a page of artwork: four reproductions in black-and-white half-tones from the Junior Drawing Class – the first illustrations of boys' work since the magazine started in 1897. The fact that the experiment was not repeated suggests that the cost was too great. In December 1929 GB's editorial took the form of an amusing playlet, which provides a good social commentary as well as an interesting historical note about the change of timetable.

The
Summer Fields Magazine

Mens Sana in Corpore Sano

| Vol. VI | DECEMBER, 1929 | No. 11 |

CONTENTS.

	PAGE
THE CONSERVATIVE PARTY	165
FOOTBALL	166
FIVES	170
SUMMER FIELDS CHAPEL	170
'THE RIVALS'	171
NEXT TERM	172
TO A DEAD BIRD	173

	PAGE
SUMMER FIELDS REGISTER	173
A NEW NOVELIST	173
'TRANSITIONAL POEM'	173
NOTES AND NEWS	174
SUMMER FIELDS-ON-SEA	176
NEWS FROM THE PUBLIC SCHOOLS	180

THE CONSERVATIVE PARTY

SCENE: The Lobby. A change has been made in the time-table.

Boy. What is it next hour, sir?

Master (sententiously). What did the Head Master give out this morning?

B. (after thought). I didn't quite hear, sir.

M. You ought to listen.

B. Yes, sir. What is it, sir?

M. Look on the board.

B. Oh! Is it up?

M. I shouldn't tell you to look if it wasn't, should I? (The Boy considers, head on one side. Evidently he is not sure. However, he goes and looks at the board.)

B. (to himself). Football colours — Special Preachers — Wanton damage — What does wanton mean, sir? (does not wait for an answer) — Carpentering, &c. — Boxing — (sighs) — What part of the board is it on, sir? I can't find it.

M. There, you ass.

B. Oh, *there!* (Looks.) I can't read what it says, sir.

M. Why, it's as plain as can be. French — F-R-E-N-C-H. What else could it be?

B. I don't know, sir. Only that didn't look like an F, to me. It looked more like a T.

M. T! Trench! Now, my poor ass, *is* there a subject called Trench?

B. No, sir. That's why I wondered, sir.

(Enter three or four more boys.)

B 2. I say, what is it next hour, anybody?

B 3. Greek. *B 2.* Greek?

B 3. Yes. Don't you remember? Old (sees master just in time) — Mr. Williams gave it out at Bible-reading. (The other boys, with accustomed tact, grin at the master, then at the speaker, to and fro, three or four times.)

B 2 (after a pause). But he didn't say *Greek*, did he?

B 3. Course he did.

B 4. That doesn't make any odds to me. I don't do Greek.

B 2. Oh lor! I shall have to go back and change my books.

M. (goaded). Of course it isn't Greek. Why don't you ever listen to anything that's given out?

B 3 (indignantly). I *did* listen, sir.

M. A fat lot of good it's done you.

Several boys. Why, sir, what is it, then?

M. French, you asses. *B 2.* *French*, sir?

M. French. French French French. Language spoken in France. French.

B 3, 4, 5, 6, &c. FRENCH, sir?

B 5. But it's always been Latin this hour, sir.

M. I know it has; but there's been a change.

B 5. (brightly) Why, sir?

M. Look here. The bell's going in two minutes. Next hour is French. It's been given out, and stuck up on the board. If any one comes with the wrong books, I'll shove him in extra drill. (Exit.)

B 5 (to the others). He can't. I'm on already. (They babble confusedly together, the word 'French' occurring frequently. The Lobby door opens. Enter another Master.)

B 1, 2, 3, 4, 5, 6, &c. (rushing up to him). Please sir — what is it next hour?

The Summer Fields Magazine, *December 1929.*

87

Two Masters from Julian Amery's album: Leonard Strong and Roger Jacques.

By contrast, July 1930 began with a very serious editorial outlining the differences in attitude towards the bringing-up of children before and after the war. Before quoting it, it is worth knowing that in 1928 Julian Amery had arrived at Summer Fields, and it was not long before he and GB were crossing swords. He retails the events in his autobiography, *Approach March*:

As a child, I had a rather overdeveloped sense of justice and of what are nowadays called 'Human Rights'. I still had to learn that life is often unjust and that this has to be accepted. At lunch one day, Mr Bolton, a rather formidable senior master, complained that I was making too much noise and told me to stop talking. I had not, as it happened, been talking at all. Springing to my feet, I replied, 'Sir, that is an outrageous statement; I have not spoken for five minutes.' My neighbours corroborated my story. Mr Bolton withdrew the charge but declined my request for an apology. I do not know whether the incident rankled with him but, anyway, a few evenings later he accused me of ragging in the dormitory. I had not, in fact, been ragging on that particular night; but, though I protested my innocence, I was given a beating. These two acts of injustice coming from a senior master called, I thought, for retaliation.

With Francis Fisher's help I proceeded to form a movement which we called 'The Anti-Authority League'. Our slogan was 'Gott Straff Authority'. At first we formed cells in the different classes. Then, when no masters were about, I addressed meetings. These were perfectly orderly. There was no violence or incitement to break the rules. I simply aired our grievances, unmasked current examples of injustice and advised my fellows to adopt an attitude of coldness and sullenness towards the masters until authority showed a change of heart. Within a few days, something like a third of the school had enrolled in the League.

It so happened – though we were quite unaware of it – that a heated debate was then going on among schoolmasters about how discipline should be enforced. Some favoured the old-fashioned "do as you're told and don't argue" formula. Others maintained that rules must be explained and justified as well as enforced. On the whole, the Summer Fields authorities leant to the more 'progressive' approach. A leading article in the Magazine that year urged masters to co-operate with the boys and to recognise that they might sometimes be wrong themselves.

Here is the bulk of the article:

The Great War has been naturally followed, in every country which it touched, by a phase of heightened sensitiveness and humanity. The mass of educated men and women, those who have it in their power to make changes, feel a fresh weight of responsibility. The prevention of cruelty to children and animals, the care of the sick and poor, the humanizing of prisons – these and many other causes have received a wealth of practical support, eloquent testimony to the working of the public conscience.

Nowhere has this general attitude of mind produced a greater effect than in the schools. The completeness and comparative suddenness of the change which has come over them since 1918 is due to several factors; but this humane sentiment has been the chief. With it went a recognition that, during the war, children had had less than their due. There was something to make up to them. Then, since 'old ideas' were all being questioned, it was thought that those who seemed to have made so many other mistakes might be wrong in their ideas of education too. The schools, which had been carrying on as best they could, were naturally somewhat disorganized. The boys, living under the shadow of war, were old beyond their years. When, once that shadow was lifted, the depleted staffs were filled by a number of young men whose nearest approach to a common characteristic was a profound distrust of army discipline, there is little wonder that the change came quickly.

These new schoolmasters . . . had no objection to discipline as such. It was the old, unreasoning discipline they disliked. 'Theirs not to reason why' – they had seen too much of that to believe in its value when doing was no longer closely connected with dying. Nor were they so sure that they invariably knew what was best for a boy because they had been in the world a few years longer than he had. The world – *their* world – was in ruins. All started equal in the new one.

So, by degrees, they began more and more to seek the boy's co-operation in the task of looking after him. The prefect system had always involved a certain amount of this, but the new tendency went farther. It spread even to the preparatory schools; and a principle, heresy to the old brigade, was everywhere proclaimed: the principle that a boy should not be asked to do a thing without first being told the reason. The only discipline worth having, declared these iconoclasts, is that which arises from a willing and intelligent co-operation between the guided and the guide.

As a result of this doctrine, the relations between boys and masters underwent a change. There was now no need for the old attitude of suspicion and veiled enmity . . . So came about the easy companionship we find today. So was learned the astonishing lesson, that the schoolmaster is not a special creation, but a human being . . .

A widespread reaction against the new system is possible but unlikely. There will always be people to support the cry for authority, control, 'a firm hand' and the like. Any reactionary with a specious tongue can raise a following. The line of least resistance has many followers; [but] the new schoolmaster has voluntarily laid aside the weapons of his predecessor. He is fighting for the spirit, not for the letter. He wishes to prevail with reason, not with pains and penalties. He is not so sure he knows everything about his boys, and so he comes to them less as a preceptor than as a companion. With his influence, his personality, with such respect and friendship as he can win by simply being himself, he does his best to make life less difficult for the boys under his care. He makes mistakes in plenty, acknowledges them freely (to the boys, if need be: why not?), and goes on trying: vigilant, quite humble-minded, and content to be judged by his results. These results are not immediate, and only time can test them; but, so far, he sees nothing to discourage him.

It would be most interesting to know who wrote that. GB was the editor: on the whole he would agree with the sentiments, but the style lacks his lightness and becomes, towards the end, sententious in a way that is not characteristic of his writing. Perhaps he got Cyril or Bobs to set out their credo. This was the last issue of the magazine in its original format. For December 1930, he began a new series and started at Volume I rather than Volume VII. Throughout the 1930s he served up the mixture largely as before but included a special feature of reminiscences by individual old boys from the earliest times; these have proved of enormous value to subsequent historians of the school.

As for the Anti-Authority League, it achieved its purpose.

From then on [Amery recalls] masters seemed to take much more trouble about me and went out of their way to make themselves pleasant. I responded to this new approach and settled down to become a useful member of the establishment.

In Amery's mid-term report for Summer 1930, GB writes:

I think that he is steadily losing the pomposity of manner which has hitherto made him rather offensive to his fellow-creatures, and that he now realises the right of others to express opinions differing from his own. This is a great step forward, & as there is no doubt as to his brains & ability he should do very well on his return.

Let us give Amery the final word. In his next chapter, which is about politics, he says:

> The reader will remember that . . . Alexander the Great, Julius Caesar and Napoleon were my heroes. Britain, I felt, needed another such leader. Was Lloyd George the man? By some accounts he had won the War. Of his oratory I had no doubt. He seemed to be getting the better of the argument then raging in the Press about Passchendale. Above all – and this was a very strong point in his favour – he was loathed by Mr Bolton.

GB with the 1932 scholars. (Standing) Viscount Ednam, D. W. K. Kay,
B. H. Middleton, H. W. L. Hartley, S. L. Newcombe;
(seated) J. L. Bell, GB, R. A. Paget-Cooke.

SUMMER FIELDS, OXFORD.

EASTER 1930.

Our respective fathers, the Rev. Dr. Williams and the Rev. E. H. Alington, are now definitely retiring from active participation in the management of the School.

It will therefore interest our parents and friends to learn that three of the present masters are joining us as partners in their stead. These are Mr. J. F. Evans (M.A., Keble College, Oxford), who has been with us for fifteen years; Mr. G. Bolton (M.A., University College, Oxford), for ten years; and Mr. R. A. K. Jacques (M.A., Brasenose College, Oxford), who was a boy at Summer Fields himself. With such experienced men to support us permanently in the supervision and conduct of affairs, we may look forward with confidence to the continued efficiency and well-being of the School.

CYRIL WILLIAMS.
A. F. ALINGTON.

Partners.

CHAPTER 6: PARTNERSHIP

GB AND JOHN EVANS, while much enjoying life at Summer Fields, had begun to feel restless, perhaps wanting to take on a school of their own. They had been thinking of moving elsewhere when the Bear had his stroke in 1928, with the results that have been explained in the last chapter. After a year or two, they once again began to make plans for a move. GB discourses on the reaction:

> Bobs now took alarm; he knew that he could never run the school jointly with Cyril. They were poles apart in their beliefs and had never got on well. So it was Bobs (as I've always understood) who went to the Doctor and said that we must be offered partnerships.
>
> Of the discreditable negotiations that followed I will say little. Time and again they were on the verge of being broken off, for the Doctor's demands were really outrageous. One must remember that in his eyes we were interlopers and he feared that we should ruin *his* school by going all modern. But we felt that we had done the School some service and that this might be recognised when we were asked to pay for the privilege of continuing that service. Doctor, however, had never failed to have his own way in the thirty-odd years since Mrs Maclaren's death, and he immensely disliked having to make concessions. Finally a sort of agreement was reached, and in January 1930 we two and Roger Jacques were enrolled as partners.

Opposite is the notice that was sent out to parents at the end of that term. To have five partners for a school of some 120 boys might seem rather extreme, especially as this decade saw a depression which affected private schools; fewer and fewer parents could afford the fees. Numbers of pupils declined throughout the 1930s, but numbers of staff needing to be paid did not. Roger Jacques recalls that one term, after the accounts had been done, the partners' share of the profits was 10/6d – decimal equivalent fifty-two pence, actual purchasing power about £25! 'Ruth and I spent it on a lunch,' he commented philosophically.

Predictably, the partners did not always get on with each other, and the whisper went round the London dinner-tables that all was not well at Summer Fields. GB describes the situation in his memoirs:

It was not a happy partnership. Too many people wanted too many different things. Our weekly meetings revealed little unanimity and after a time were apt to resolve themselves into a monologue by John on the iniquities of his Latin form while the rest of us thought our own thoughts. My particular fault, a serious one, was that I was so happy in my own ploys of V Form, Soccer and Cubicles that I didn't bother enough about what was going on around me.

GB had certainly done his best to make Cubicles a happy place, and many old boys of that period remember with pleasure his evening readings of Wodehouse and his rising betimes in the summer to take them for an early morning swim in the river – a nice variant on the cold bath! At first he had had to guess at most of his duties, but he soon came to find it a congenial job. Not living on the spot, he had to trust public opinion and a set of prefects. Hugh Stubbs recalls that on the whole this system worked: boys were terrified of the Cubicles prefects, whose regular gambit was to say in portentous tones, "I *think* you'd better report yourself to GB in the morning." Then, after having allowed a period of anguish, they would tiptoe round and whisper, "It's all right: you needn't report yourself really."

GB's way of looking at the situation was that, if he read to them nearly every night when they were abed, it was up to them to refrain from ragging when he was not there. In his sixteen years in charge of Cubicles he had little trouble.

Having a statistical mind of a rather silly sort, I tried to calculate how many words I had read to Cubicles over the years, and I arrived at the impressive total of twenty million. Those were the days of Wodehouse at his best, the vintage years of *Right Ho, Jeeves*, of *Summer Lightning*, of *Leave It To Psmith* and of *Money For Nothing*, and the shouts of laughter that rang round Cubicles still linger gratefully on the ear. Once, on the first night of term, I read a brand new Jeeves story from the *Strand* ('Jeeves and the Old School Chum'): anyone coming in would have thought it was the last night of term, for we laughed ourselves nearly silly.

The earlier Wodehouse stories were not neglected. *Mike and Psmith* had been the joy of my own boyhood; there were *Love among the Chickens*, *Something Fresh*, *The Little Nugget*, *The Girl on the Boat* and many another. Then there were W. W. Jacobs, Anthony Hope, *Vice Versa*, *The Human Boy*, the Richard Hannay stories, A. A. Milne's *Punch* stories and one or two experiments, not all of which came off. Stevenson, for instance, is not easy to read aloud, and I found Conan Doyle impossible. Once, to my horror, I found a boy who had never heard of *The Jungle Book*; so Kipling was duly 'plugged' for some time, but I could not read aloud the end of the *Drums of the Fore and Aft*.

What was once Cubicles is now the school library. In the second bay on the left, among the other red leather Macmillan pocket editions of Kipling is *Life's Handicap*, inscribed 'G. Bolton, July 29, 1912, with best wishes d.d. Percy G. Exham.' A similar edition of *Wee Willie Winkie* contains 'The Drums of the Fore and Aft'.

On the subject of Conan Doyle, either he or Sapper, author of the Bulldog Drummond stories, was frequently held up to ridicule by GB for a notable howler of pretentiously mistaken English: '"Whom can it have been?" I cried.'

Though the usage of 'whom' is very much in decline in the early twenty-first century, the same howler appeared in *The Times* in July 1998, where a writer mentioned 'biographers whom, as he intended, transmitted his words to the public'. *Plus ça change . . .*

According to Christopher Lee, GB also sometimes read M. R. James ghost stories. A pleasing circularity occurs here in that Brian Johnston, reminiscing for *Eton Voices*, says, "I was very lucky because I often went to supper with Monty James, who was the Provost, and he used to read P. G. Wodehouse; he hardly ever got through a page because he used to laugh so much!"

Christopher Lee was in Fifth Form, from 1934 to 1936, and had vivid memories of GB.

Christopher Lee.

What we knew of the Classics was riveted home by the force of his personality. He loved them, and love to him meant an all-round muscular effort of the brain. He had no patience with slackers and he believed God had averted His face from those who saw no purpose in the Classics.

In fact, as we know, it is probable that GB did not believe in God: it might have been more concordant to say 'the gods'.

Lee goes on to discuss GB's appearance, including 'totally white' hair, 'the result of shell-shock in the Great War'; so there is that myth, already established in the 1930s.

For the same reason, he had a volatile temper. He boiled over very easily. He was absurdly easy to provoke and, since he had a passionate dislike of Lloyd George and all he stood for, a boy had only to ask him a mild question about the little Welsh wizard to see him work himself up into a rage . . . [1]

All honour to his memory. I write this despite my special dislike of one of his classroom ploys, which was neither bad-tempered nor witty, but simply schoolmaster's beastly. For a minor solecism in a Latin construe he would cry 'Tweaks!' and the boys on either side of the offender would fall upon him pinching him. For a significant lapse in taste of grammatical understanding he would shout 'Roots!' and everybody near enough would pull the malefactor's hair.

This was indeed beastly, and one cannot excuse it; but it should be borne in mind that at Summer Fields, and no doubt other schools, hair-pulling and pinching were common punishments among prefects and staff at that time and even post-war.

Despite the horrors of Roots and Tweaks, Lee 'wanted to please GB in particular. I thought I must be a run-machine at Cricket. I thought I should be a charging centre forward on the football field [GB put him firmly in goal!]. I thought I should bowl very fast.' Here GB, a slow bowler, could not be a role model; so Lee decided to imitate the dashing young school secretary, Eric Bowtell, who arrived in 1930 and made an impressive impact on Summer Fields cricket and soccer for the next three decades.

Mr Bowtell's action is not seen often on cricket grounds: one rotates one's arm not once, but twice, before releasing the ball, lending a windmill appearance to the movement which certainly surprises and may well mesmerize the batsman, so that one delivers the ball off the wrong foot. This is also a valuable piece of deception; on the other hand, one hasn't quite the control a normal action gives . . . I found it hard to release the ball at the right moment. I built up terrifically and unwound at the crease with panache: the fielders and batsmen would all stare intently at the spot they supposed the ball should land. Then nothing would materialise. A shout of derisive applause from the spectators fifty yards behind me would . . . signify the ball had gone backwards at speed to the boundary.

As a batsman, I made most of my runs in the nets. I was too flash for a long innings. I was always promising something amazing but out in the middle I let it go. 'Keep your eye on the ball and not on the spectators,' said GB, going to the heart of the matter [but] I would rather be out playing a stylish stroke than stay in with a bad one. It's an attitude that makes neither runs nor friends.

Eric Bowtell remembers playing squash with GB and also making use of his 'flighted twisters' when he was running the North Oxford cricket team.

Eric Bowtell.

One of my treasured memories was when the club fielded two SF Headmasters – John Evans, an extremely stylish bat joining GB to bring a touch of class with his Authentics blazer. During my 30-odd years at the School I made films of Summer Fields life, and I remember getting GB to act in a sketch delivering 'six of the best'. Sadly, realism was not achieved as neither actor could play it straight – which did not trouble the 'house full' audience in New Room, the humorous glint in GB's eye being the high spot of the film. It was a great première.

Eric Bowtell's recollections include GB on Sports Day as a "sleek figure in a smart suit, charming mums and winning the admiration of the dads as they probed about their sons' progress. He was a fine character and a perfect gentleman."

GB was indeed critical of ungentlemanliness in others:

> Nobody to whom Oxford cricket means anything can look back on the 1930 season without feeling an impotent anger at the way in which Fortune's gifts were squandered. The season opened with the brightest of prospects: at its close Oxford had touched the depths of humiliation. 'Tragic', said some, but the word will not do. Tragedy begins when something fine and noble suffers frustration: the main feature of ancient tragedy was there – the chastisement of *Hubris* – but fineness and nobility were not among the qualities of that side.
>
> In the last decade before Hitler's war – a terrifying and shameful period in our history – a new and unwelcome spirit manifested itself in Sport. It was the spirit of 'If I can't win, you shan't' and it was disturbingly powerful in football of both codes and in top-class cricket. Happily, University cricket was largely unaffected; not entirely, for there was the 'body-line' bowling by Cambridge in 1933 which led to heated discussions and caused a well-known Cambridge player to say, 'I could not feel proud of my University that day'. But for the most part, though there seemed to be an added grimness in the struggle, the University cricket matches were played in the old spirit.

The 1930s was an unhappy decade, and not least for prep schools, many of which closed as the general depression bit deep into parents' pockets. In Summer Fields' case, this was compounded by the knowledge, which inevitably got about, that the partners were at variance. Cyril did not appeal to all the parents, either. Those who liked him liked him a lot, but he had an unfortunate manner and had ruffled many feathers in the days before he was headmaster.

Despite the strife and uncertainty, GB was, as he said, extremely happy. This was probably the decade that saw him at the height of his powers, really getting to grips with Fifth Form and enjoying running the soccer. The period 1934–7 was particularly good in terms of the latter, with the peak being the 1936 season under the captaincy of Brian Straton-Ferrier, who has left this memorable account of the final game of an undefeated season:

> On Saturday, 5th December 1936, we played Horris Hill at home, the last match of the season. So far we were unbeaten. Cothill – it would have to be Cothill – had managed to draw with us. Gerald Seager had had one of his very rare off- days and he missed a couple of sitters. GB swore he'd never seen anything like it since the famous day when David James skied the ball over the cross-bar from five yards in front of an open goal.
>
> (The evil that boys did lived after them. Poor David James, immortalized for generations by this single oft-told incident. Eternal infamy in this brief moment of zealous excess. The Lawson-Clauson gang [1933 Fifth Form: see page 82] at least must have maintained a high standard of turpitude over a long period to win *their* enduring reputation as the worst Fifth Form of all time.)
>
> None of us had been able to concentrate during that last week, and I was afraid lest one of the side should earn himself a whacking or be put in Black

Football 1st XI, 1936: 'Invicti'.
(Standing) R. H. Dobson, M. J. Berry, T. A. S. Carlyon, E. B. Close;
(seated) T. H. Barclay, Hon. J. L. Mackay, B. I. Straton-Ferrier, W. M. Savery,
G. E. Seager; (on the ground) D. O'R Dickey, J. W. Hext.

David James, from the rugby XV, 1932 (see page 82).

Book 2 for inattention, with disastrous effects on morale. In the event nobody got so much as a double-sided copy . . . I think none of the staff dared risk Boltosh's[2] wrath by demoralizing any of his precious First Eleven. So Tark's gumpher-rod remained in its drawer, and Liz Lysaght's supply of History Picture sticks remained high.

In Fifth Form the tension was unbearable. That long, bony finger, and the jumbo yellow pencil, probed around the class much as usual, pausing now and then as one of us, too late, remembered the meaning of the vocab-book word a fraction of a second before it passed the lips of the next in line, while the familiar verse was sonorously repeated, as if for the first time:

> The moving finger writes, and having writ
> Moves on, nor all thy piety nor wit
>   Shall lure it back to cancel half a line
> Nor all thy tears wash out one word of it.

But Saturday's match was in the forefront of all minds, and the whole of ancient literature seemed crammed with subtle references to the impending decisive battle. On the Friday evening we sang the psalm usually reserved for the day before Common E.: 'The ploughers ploughed along my back and made long furrows.' It wished us good luck in the name of the Lord. And finally Saturday came.

A few hurried last-minute conferences, and the plan of campaign was complete. 'We must have a goal *quickly*,' GB said for the umpteenth time, 'so get in there with everything you've got and score ὡς ταχίστα . . . !'[3]

So there we were, trotting on to the field at last, neat adrenalin pumping through our veins. There was GB, his match-stick legs in long blue shorts and those crazy boots of his, his face trying desperately to register a referee's impartiality, and refusing to talk to us now we were under starter's orders. He looked grim, tired.

How that gaunt figure dominated my five years! I loved and revered him, and was terribly afraid of him, and now I wanted this triumph more, I think, for his sake than for ours.

GB blew his whistle and we kicked off. What immediately happened is a blur, but about thirty seconds later an image like a photograph impinged indelibly on my mind. In this picture we are attacking Horris Hill's goal, and Gerald Seager is poised high in the air like Nijinsky among a crowd of defenders, his clever head having found a good centre from the left wing. He deflected it in a high, slow lob towards the goalkeeper (a boy called Guy Lister: I knew him in the holidays). The goalie fumbled. The ball dropped on the line. He, two Horris Hill full backs, Gerald, Tommy Carlyon and I reached it about the same time. There was a great impact, and a moment later there were the two full backs, Guy Lister, ball and all in a heap at the back of the net.

I shall never forget Geoffrey Bolton's face as he came running up after blowing his whistle to register a goal. He was laughing, laughing in great uncontrollable giggles of glee, all pretence of judicial calm abandoned in this one moment of overwhelming victory.

For it was all over, and we knew it, and they knew it. We won quite easily after that. GB gave me a silver pencil engraved with the single word *Invictus*. I don't think I ever valued anything so much. It broke my heart when I lost it in my first term at Harrow.

The next year, 1937, was a significant one in the world of Oxford cricket:

> The season started with a great win over Gloucester . . . Defeat by Yorkshire was followed by a run of draws, the most noticeable of which was that with the New Zealanders . . . Included in the New Zealand side was a youth under twenty years of age, his name Martin Paterson Donnelly. One day he would be seen in the Parks again.

Martin Donnelly.

M. P. Donnelly (born in November 1917) was generally agreed to be the most exciting and elegant left-hand batsman in the years after the war. As well as being a superb batsman and fielder, he was a rugby international, playing against Ireland in 1946–7. He played cricket for Wellington, Canterbury, New Zealand, Oxford, and briefly Middlesex and Warwickshire. The zenith of his career was the 1949 New Zealand tour of England, in which he made 206 in the Lord's test. He then gave up cricket for business, and retired to Australia. GB's article on him in the *Barclay's Book of Cricketers* ends:

Bare figures can give no idea of the electric atmosphere in the Parks when that short, sturdy figure went in to bat. A lucky spectator might have half an hour to spare between, say, a lecture at Keble and a tutorial in Parks Road. In that half-hour he might well see Donnelly hit 9 boundaries, each from a different stroke. Most exquisite of all would be the late cut and the straight drive; there would be an on-drive, a square leg-hit, a devastating hook, perhaps a rustic pull worthy of George Hirst. There was not a stroke of which Donnelly was not the master. If Oxford were fielding, the spectator's eyes would turn to cover-point. There have been great covers in cricket's history – Royle, Jessop, S. E. Gregory, Hobbs, John Gunn – but few greater than Donnelly. He was equally brilliant in anticipation, in pick-up and in throw. Equable of temper, modest, friendly and possessing a great gift of fun, Martin Donnelly was as popular off the field as on it. His cricket career was short: memories of it will endure.

The 1920s and 1930s were the heyday of the D'Oyly Carte Opera Company, and GB steeped himself in the productions, buying the newly minted 78rpm records of Leo Sheffield, Sydney Granville, Derek Oldham, Bertha Lewis and his great hero, Henry Lytton. Lytton was a veteran of the company, having appeared with them at the age of seventeen in Glasgow in 1884. He played all the Gilbert and Sullivan baritone roles in his time, but soon took the leading 'funny men', which he sustained until 1932. He wrote two books of memoirs, *The Secrets of a Savoyard* and *A Wandering Minstrel*, and was knighted for services to the stage in 1930. GB collected innumerable editions of the Savoy libretti, and maintained that the illustrations in the Russell Flint editions clearly featured Lytton. He took friends and pupils, such as Jimmy Bell, to the operas at the Savoy in the holidays – Rupert D'Oyly Carte was, incidentally, an Old Summerfieldian – and there were regular parties when the company came to the New Theatre at Oxford. GB knew two members of the company, Leslie Rands and Marjorie Eyre, personally, as they were friends of Pat Marston. Like many married couples in the theatre, they had one child, who was cared for with other children of the company by a foster-mother in Brighton.

During all this time, GB was playing holiday cricket for the Sussex Martlets; he was on the committee by now, and one of their match managers. The club had had a bad patch in the 1920s, but by the mid-1930s their fixture list was rapidly expanding.

Of all our opponents there is no doubt which was the toughest nut to crack. The Old Brightonians were a side that may not have had a superior in club cricket anywhere – a host of fine cricketers, who usually administered tremendous thrashings to their opponents and most of all to the Martlets. They were a grand side to play against, and to have raised and skippered the first Martlets side to beat them gave me the most genuine thrill of my cricket career.

He also played in the Easter holidays for the Cryptics, which he joined in 1931, being officially elected a member in January 1932. This club comprised mainly schoolmasters, many of whom were former blues. Between the wars they regularly spent a week in both Oxford and Cambridge playing college

Marjorie Eyre and Leslie Rands in The Sorcerer.

sides. GB batted No. 11 for them and was a useful change bowler; he played for them throughout the 1930s, his best season being 1934, when he took twenty-one wickets at an average of 8.38.

It was in this year that the number of boys at Summer Fields sank below 100 for the first time since Mrs Maclaren's days. The decline continued slowly, and in 1937 Cyril, who had been finding his position difficult, announced that he would resign.

Bobs summoned the other partners to Mayfield and outlined fully and frankly what he intended his policy to be. He and Gill had 'modern' ideas, and it became clear to JFE and GB that the whole character of Summer Fields was about to change in ways that they could not countenance. The final upshot of a spate of resignations, counter-resignations and mind-changing was that Bobs decided to leave, in order to avoid further discord (the Doctor, for instance, would never have tolerated his plans for the 'new' Summer Fields). GB could sympathise with him in some ways, but not with his views. 'He had a deep love for Summer Fields, but an equally deep dislike for much of what it stood for, and compromise was not really possible.'

For the time-being Cyril withdrew his resignation, and for two more uneasy years the machine continued to function. In 1939 he decided that he really had had enough and would leave at the end of the summer. Roger Jacques also chose this moment to go elsewhere; so JFE and GB were left to take on the school in September 1939 with, as they expected, some eighty boys. As headmaster, John decided to leave Cottage and go to live in 'the Front'; so GB gave up Cubicles and moved from Front Lodge to Cottage.

Like most people in Britain in 1939, those at Summer Fields were not really expecting war; but they had at least taken the precaution of building a serviceable, though not enormous, air-raid shelter. This was to come into use all too soon.

Notes:

1. A good example of GB's bigotry and wit is his reputed answer to somebody who told him that Wales was playing France at rugby: "I hope they both lose!" It is also worth mentioning here that when, sixty years later, Christopher Lee acted an ancient classical master in the film *A Feast at Midnight*, there was a distinct touch of GB in his portrayal, particularly his gauntness and inflammability.
2. Brian Straton-Ferrier says that he wrote 'Bollosh', the current nickname for GB, but that Richard Usborne edited it as 'Boltosh'. The latter ties up with GB's fondness for the expression 'tosh' to describe either rubbishy bowling or worthless nonsense, especially in juvenile attempts at Latin prose. 'Tark' was John Evans; the 'gumpher-rod' was presumably some sort of cane. Lysaght produced a series of 'history pictures' in collaboration with L. A. G. Strong, as visual aids to his lessons; the sticks would be used as pointers or as spindles round which to wrap the pictures when not in use; but they could also be used for chastisement!
3. ὡς τάχιστα is the Greek equivalent of the Latin *quam celerrime*, or perhaps in this context *quam primum*, meaning 'as quickly as possible'.

The 1940 school photograph, showing the boost to numbers of both boys and staff given by the advent of Farnborough. Christopher Slade, 1st scholar at Eton and future Chairman of the Summer Fields Governors, sits between JFE and GB.

SUMMER FIELDS

NEAR OXFORD

School Roll, Summer 1940

CLASSICAL ORDER

UPPER SCHOOL

FIFTH FORM

P L A I.I.I. C. J. Slade, ma. 12.11
P L A I.I.I. J. D. Bethune. 13.8
L A I.I.I. F. P. E. Gardner. 11.10
P L A 2.I.I. M. J. Seely. 13.8
A I.I.I. O. D. H. Clauson. 13.0
P L A I.I.I. M. I. Anderson, ma. 13.2
L A 2.I.I. F. D. Clarke. 13.8
L A I.I.I. C. P. Barker. 12.9

UPPER REMOVE

L A I.2.I. H. A. S. Murray. 12.9
A I.2.I. R. A. P. Burrill, ma. 13.0
A 2.2.I. D. C. Bull, ma. 13.3
A 2.2.I. D. Churchill-Davidson. 13.0
L A 2.2.I. I. P. Guinness, ma. 12.8
A 2.2.I. J. G. Macnee. 12.4
A 2.I.I. F. C. Chute. 11.2
A 2.2.I. W. I. B. Haine. 12.7
A I.2.I. C. J. Heywood. 11.10

LOWER REMOVE

L B I.I.I. M. M. Cahill. 12.7
B I.I.I. H. R. Hall. 12.7
*P L B I.I.I. C. Brotherton-Ratcliffe. 13.6
B 2.I.I. J. Crawshay-Williams. 11.7
B I.I.I. M. B. Noble, ma. 13.4
B 2.I.I. F. A. M. Cripps. 10.10
B I.I.I. J. W. Shaw Stewart. 11.3
B I.I.I. A. M. Mackrill. 12.11
L B I.I.I. T. N. Hainault. 12.10

UPPER FOURTH

B 2.I.I. N. A. S. Barrett. 13.2
B 2.I.I. R. D. Hambleton. 12.10
B I.I.2. D. C. Bakirgian. 12.6
B 2.I.2. D. G. H. Marsden. 10.5
B 2.2.I. R. T. Salisbury. 12.9
B 3.2.2. M. Winsor-Cundell. 11.7
B I.2.2. A. J. L. Lloyd. 11.0
B 2.2.2. A. M. Stroumillo. 11.3

MIDDLE FOURTH

B 2.2.2. D. J. S. Wilkinson. 11.9
B 3.2.2. D. A. Keown-Boyd. 12.3
B 3.3.2. R. P. Clark-Turner. 11.11
B I.2.I. C. M. Campbell. 13.4
B 3.2.2. A. Harvey. 13.0
B 3.2.2. J. P. Hudson. 10.10
B 3.2.2. P. J. E. Hubbard 11.0
B 3.I.I. J. R. Chanter. 10.9

LOWER FOURTH

B 3.2.2. D. N. Spurrier. 13.2
L B 4.3.2. A. F. Cottier. 12.3
B 2.2.3. H. M. D. Norton. 10.3
B 3.3.3. T. I. Dale-Harris. 11.0
B 2.3.3. G. H. R. Burrill, mi. 11.3
B 4.2.2. D. L. Roberts, ma. 12.4
B 3.2.3. V. P. Lemay. 11.0

SHELL

B 3.3.3. R. T. J. Tuck. 9.11
B 4.3.3. W. L. Bull, mi. 11.0
B 3.2.3. P. G. P. D. Fullerton. 10.3
B 4.3.3. H. F. Grosvenor. 12.6
B 4.3.3. A. E. Gather. 11.0
B 4.3.3. J. B. Guinness, mi. 10.1
B 4.3.3. J. P. Slade, mi. 9.11
B 4.3.3. P. S. F. Noble, mi. 10.11

LOWER SCHOOL

UPPER THIRD

C I.2.2. J. A. Garland. 11.3
C 2.2.I. R. B. Anderson, mi. . 11.5
C I.I.2. N. F. Hirsch. 10.1
C I.I.I. J. L. Johnstone. 11.9
C I.I.I. C. M. Mosselmans. 11.1
C 2.I.I. M. T. Coller. 10.6
C I.I.I. A. Cartwright. 9.10
C 2.I.2. S. Lezard. 10.6
C I.I.I. J. G. R. Alington. 11.1

LOWER THIRD

C I.I.I. J. B. Worsley. 11.4
C I.I.2. D. R. W. Lawrence. 11.0
C 2.2.I. E. W. A. Sanford. 10.11
C 2.2.I. G. A. R. Fillingham. 10.7
C I.2.I. A. D. Y. Naylor-Leyland. 10.11
C I.2.I. A. J. W. Lewis. 10.10
C I.2.I. P. J. R. Spira. 10.2
C 2.2.2. P. H. G. Bengough. 10.11

UPPER SECOND

C 2.3.2. D. S. Salt, ma. 9.11
C 2.3.I. E. F. Grey, ma. 10.0
C 3.2.2. T. D. Brinton. 10.3
C I.I.I. H. P. G. Hinde, ma. 10.6
C 3.3.2. J. B. Anderson, mus. 9.11
C 2.2.2. P. W. B. Freeman. 9.8
C 3.3.2. C. Gascoigne. 10.6

LOWER SECOND

C 2.3.2. C. de C. P. Paynter. 9.9
C 3.3.3. N. S. G. Hinde, mi. 9.0
C 2.3.2. M. J. R. Gould. 10.3
C 3.3.2. R. D. Grey, mi. 8.11
C 3.2.2. D. W. T. Mackenzie. 10.9
C 3.3.2. P. L. Strong. 8.4
C 3.3.3. A. H. Salt, mi. 8.7
C 3.4.3. E. I. Illingworth-Law. 10.9
C 3.2.I. M. D. M. Keddie. 10.11
C 3.3.2. N. Ades. 10.6

FIRST FORM

C 4.4.3. E. D. Moylan. 8.10
C 4.4.3. J. D. Thicknesse. 8.9
C 4.3.3. A. Florescu 7.11
C 4.4.3. M. J. D. Player. 8.9
C 4.3.3. R. D. G. Elliott. 8.6
C 3.3.3. *H. J. F. Lawson.* 8.8
C 4.4.3. *P. L. Roberts, mi.* 8.7
C 4.4.3. *O. F. W. Fisher.* 7.4

P Prefect.   * Captain of Cricket.   L League Leader.
The first number before a boy's name shows his Division in Mathematics; the second his Division in French; and the third his Division in English. The age of each boy follows his name. New boys' names are in italic.
This Term ends on Wednesday, JULY 31. London Train arrives Paddington at 10.5 a.m.
Next Term begins on Wednesday, SEPTEMBER 25.

CHAPTER 7: WAR AGAIN

JOHN EVANS stayed at Summer Fields during the summer holidays of 1939 to supervise his move from Cottage to House. GB went off to play cricket as usual, but returned on 1st September, 'very much wondering if there would be a school or not'. They decided in fact to begin the term as early as possible, even though the enormous work of blacking-out had barely started, and GB went off in his car to round up a quorum of domestic staff. He spent the rest of the time in moving his effects from Front Lodge, where he had lived for twenty years, to Cottage, where he was to spend another seventeen. He found it a real wrench to leave Cubicles, but had too much to do to have time for being homesick.

He was indeed at this time in charge of:

Fifth Form	The boys' pocket money
Cottage	The Buzzer (school shop)
Soccer	The Library
Squash	The timetable
The magazine	The leagues

He gave up the Library fairly soon, not without regret, but continued to do all the others till well after the war. The magazine was not published between 1942 and 1944 because of the paper shortage, but he had to keep a record, which duly appeared in a much condensed form in 1944.

In September 1939, the school roll numbered barely eighty, and of these some twelve were caught overseas; but the arrival of E. K. Stephenson with four masters and twenty boys from Farnborough swelled the numbers, and for a brief while there was actually a plethora of teaching staff. But one by one the young masters (including Pat Savage) were called up, and many failed to return. One of GB's most poignant memories of the summer of 1939 is of going to Oxford one Sunday morning to clinch the appointment of Budge Dixon, the Oxford cricket captain, and (for 1940) of Hugh Davies, captain-elect of soccer. Dixon spent six weeks at the school before joining the RAF, and was killed in the war; Davies died in a German prison camp.

Of the four masters who were due to join the staff in 1939, only Patrick Savage survived the war. He gives an interesting account of the two headmasters:

JFE's nickname among the boys was Ticky; GB didn't seem to have a nickname[1], though, on one occasion when he appeared in a duffel coat on a chilly December evening, I do remember hearing a boy murmur, 'Here comes Old Father Advent!' It had been a friendly convention at Summer Fields that masters should call each other by their christian names; but GB was always GB and never Geoffrey, except to Sussex Martlets and others in cricketing circles. He was not amused when his spindly handwriting – never easy to read – led to his getting a letter addressed to Guy Bottom Esq.

John never seemed to get old. His hair was quite dark until the very end. GB never looked young: his hair had gone white at an early age. It certainly helped with the discipline. Even his approach to the Classics was most of the time far severer than what I had been used to at Westminster. Nor could I share his devotion to P. G. Wodehouse or Gilbert & Sullivan – or indeed cricket. But I admired and liked him greatly – especially as a teacher: one of the Very Greatest.

In 1940 what was left of Summer Fields St Leonard's arrived with Ken and Kitty Barber (she was Dr Williams' daughter) and three masters. In 1942 came a small body from St Cyprian's, Eastbourne, with their headmaster, Bill Tomlinson, and his wife, Bud. This brought the numbers up to 120, and Mayfield was reopened to house the Tomlinsons and some boys. GB was on the friendliest of terms with them, and used to visit Mayfield frequently; Bud made him a birthday cake annually on 30th July.

The teaching staff was rapidly whittled down by call-ups, so that for most of the war it consisted of JFE, GB, Lysaght, Ralph Robinson, and the Miss Hills; A. W. H. ('Stodgy') Thomson from Farnborough; and Ken Barber, David Mansel-Carey, D. Standring and M. P. Dobson from St Leonard's; others came and went. There is an amusing cartoon of the staff from 1943 drawn by Julian Slade, who evidently had a gift for caricature as well as musical composition. He had been very frightened of GB at first:

> to a small boy he cut a fearsome figure and, although his bark was undoubtedly worse than his bite, it could be an extremely alarming bark.
>
> It was he who first introduced me to the world of J. M. Barrie. *Peter Pan*, of course, I already knew through annual Christmas treats, but the other plays were a revelation. I think I liked the stage directions best and I was never so thrilled as when my mother gave me a *Complete Works* for my twelfth birthday. GB was also responsible for enthusing me with his rather surprising love of Gilbert and Sullivan. He had a large selection of D'Oyly Carte records, and it was a great treat to be invited to Cottage to listen to them. The works of these masters made an indelible impression on my youthful mind, and I have no doubt that their influence did much to inspire the musical plays I was later to write.
>
> GB also kept a close eye on my reading and, if he were ever to catch me with a copy of *Biggles Flies North*, he would tear it out of my hands and substitute *The Caravaners* by the author of *Elizabeth and Her German Garden*, or anything else he regarded as 'literature' rather than 'rubbish'.

108

Ken and Kitty Barber; he was headmaster of Summer Fields St Leonard's from 1929 to 1950; she was Dr Williams' daughter.

Bill and Bud Tomlinson, with their children.

Julian Slade.

Given the variety of the staff, GB found it remarkable that the school had some very successful scholastic years (notably 1941, 1943 and 1946) and quite reasonable success at games.

Christopher Slade, Julian's elder brother, who also joined the school from Farnborough, has described the differences between the two schools as they struck an intelligent twelve-year-old; more especially, he gives an account of life in Fifth Form:

> Life at Summer Fields was rather more regimented than it had been at Farnborough; above all, there was a far more stringent scholastic programme. To join Fifth Form under GB was, to begin with, a daunting experience. The cane no longer hung on the end of his desk, as we were told it had done only a few years before. However, his gaunt, hollow-eyed and skeletal presence, his quick temper and his bellow were alarming, until one came to appreciate his complete dedication to the school and, beneath a gruff exterior, his almost infinite kindness to those whom he considered worthy citizens – and there were many of them.
>
> Though no great scholar himself, he was a marvellous teacher of the classics. We were given our grammar or vocabulary to learn before breakfast, at breakfast itself, and at other convenient gaps in the working day. But once we had more or less learned it, he devised the most imaginative ways of testing us. These included frequent cricket matches between the counties, when a mistake would cost the batting side a wicket. These matches were fun, save when the wrong side (Sussex!) lost and GB's disappointment and displeasure were all too clear.
>
> He taught us to write simple Latin and Greek Prose and to translate into English, avoiding more than the minimum number of clichés. 'Down with parrot mentality!' was one of his favourite phrases, and he meant it. After the scholarship exams, in the middle of the summer term he introduced us to Homer with infectious enthusiasm. The school was often accused of 'cramming'; so far as he was concerned, the accusation would have been quite unjust.

110

Cartoon of the Staff by Julian Slade.

Oxford was not bombed; there was at one stage fear of 'Baedeker raids' directed at cultural centres, but they never materialised. At first, though, when the sirens went, the boys were made to go down to the air-raid shelter. This practice was soon abandoned, however; the risk of pneumonia was at least as great as that of being hit. The shelter was used in the winter of 1940/1, when evening alarms were sounded at about six o'clock. Its end compartment was reserved for Fifth Form; they and GB plodded on with their *Borva Notes, Anglice Reddenda* or whatever, winding up as a rule with a Jacobs or Wodehouse story. Conditions must have been cramped and stuffy with some hundred boys and two dozen staff (teaching, matronal and domestic) crammed into a thin tube about as long as a cricket pitch.

University cricket was suspended during the war, but GB found some opportunities for cricket apart from at Summer Fields. Charles Hossell, who later joined the Summer Fields teaching staff, was a boy at St Edward's during the war.

> I first met GB in 1943 when he used to come over to Teddies and umpire some school matches and bowl in the nets. In those war years all the young staff were in the services, so we boys had to be our own coaches, and you can imagine what a joy it was to have expert batting practice. He was usually accompanied by Bill Tomlinson, who had played for Derbyshire and got a cricket blue at Cambridge in 1923; the combination of GB's slow left arm and Bill's medium quick right arm was brilliant. They coached us without appearing to do so and were a major reason for the successful St Edward's cricket side in 1944, which included Derek Henderson and Mike Womersley, both of whom were briefly on the staff at Summer Fields, while waiting to go up to Trinity.

Mike went on to a successful business career and became chairman of the governors at the Dragon School; Derek founded, and ran for over thirty years, Moor Park, a Roman Catholic prep school in a lovely setting near Ludlow.

The nuisance of air-raid alerts ceased in 1941, and the shelter was not used thereafter; it survived, an empty mound of mystery, until 1978, when it was flattened to make way for the new teaching block, suitably to be called Bolton. The school 'carried on', never free from anxiety and always with too much to do, but yet with a surprising lack of interruption. The pestilent winters of 1940/1/2 gave way to an improvement after Alamein, when the school bell, silent since Dunkirk, was allowed to be rung one celebratory Sunday. John and GB spent most of their holidays at the school: "it wasn't much fun, but we thought it best to be on hand".

GB was at Eton with the scholarship candidates when the Normandy Landings occurred. The next year, once he had seen the boys off for their post-scholarship weekend at home, he took the train to Brighton, got his car out of storage and drove it back to Summer Fields. This was his pre-war Lanchester, and he bought a new one a few years later, the 1953 14-h.p., four-cylinder Leda.

A trio of St Edward's cricketers who went on to Oxford and taught at Summer Fields: Charles Hossell, Mike Womersley and Derek Henderson. The fourth master in this picture is Harold Clayton, and the boys are James Fox, George Phillipson, Robin Borthwick and Richard White.

*Pat Savage was clever in catching this moment when GB and three
hopeful candidates for the Eton Scholarship were loading
up the Lanchester before departing.*

GB found life at Cottage rather more strenuous than being in charge of
Cubicles. There was the added responsibility of living on the spot; he had
much more room than he had had at Front Lodge, but Cottage (which Pat
Savage suggested was "the only three-storey cottage in existence") was not a
very comfortable building. It had been built c.1905 for the Gmelins, with
more haste than consideration of amenities. It had no damp course – which
GB did not discover until after some of his books were ruined. All the windows
faced east or west. During Double Summer Time, therefore, he had to get up
in the chill of what was really 4 a.m., while at the end of the day the sun
poured into his sitting room at bedtime.

Cottage.

The war was characterised by the difficulty of obtaining domestic staff, but there was a piece of luck in the arrival of Miss Morgan, who stayed almost until the end of GB's time at Cottage. She was sixty when she arrived and the work was more than she should have had to cope with alone, but she could never keep a maid for long, so exacting were her standards. She was never late, the house was kept spotlessly clean, and she was forever thinking of something to increase the comfort of the boys or masters. GB worshipped her and, according to him, the boys adored her, though "she routed them round occasionally".

From GB's *History of the O.U.C.C.*, 'Return to Paradise II'; 1946–51:

On a cold April day in 1946 cricket returned to the Parks. Among those assembled in the pavilion to see the first ball were three men, any of whom, if asked 'Who is sure to be there today?' would have named the other two.[2] It did not seem possible that the nightmare was over at last and, as they shivered in their great coats, the watchers were as thrilled as children at their first party. One of them, who spent most of his time in Oxford, had occasionally visited the Parks in the war years to look at the ground and perhaps murmur, "Quousque, Domine?" But one day he had seen a horrid thing. Across the sacred sward had been placed a series of objects like those used for 'yard cricket' at some Public Schools. These, it appeared, were for baseball practice. Steeling himself, the watcher took post near one of these objects; he had been told that to compare baseball to rounders was the supreme insult and he wanted to see for himself. Forth strode a stocky figure, rather like Maurice Leyland, but there was no white rose on the cap that he wore askew. He omitted to take guard, but that was of no consequence, for the bowler (or what you will) sent down a number of fast sneaks outside the off stump. Leyland paid no heed to these, but as soon as one was moderately pitched up he tried a cow-shot and was caught at mid-on. The watcher fled and came that way no more until this joyful April morning . . .

There was one great difference between 1919 and 1946. In 1919, as we said earlier, we who survived were anxious to go on where we had left off, confident that life would return automatically to the normal. In 1946 there were no such illusions. Life could never be the same again and the future looked pretty grim. So did Oxford itself: it was not (thank God) war-scarred, but it was appallingly shabby. The silent fingers which still pointed to Heaven were badly in need of a wash. Moreover, accommodation was at a premium. The undergraduate no longer wanted a room for himself: he wanted rooms for his wife and children and he had to put up with what he could get. Perhaps the strangest sight of all, and by no means the least attractive, was the line of prams drawn up behind the nets while practice was going on. The occupants, albeit unconsciously, were at least imbibing first principles at the earliest possible age!

This pleasure at the sight of the prams, no doubt accompanied by nannies or mothers, is further evidence that GB enjoyed the company of both babies and women. David Kidd-May recalls an occasion a few years later when he and his wife, Jo, were living in Front Lodge and had invited GB over for a glass of sherry. Among the company was the Kidd-Mays' two-year-old daughter, Sarah-Jane. GB sat by her, dipped his fingertip in his glass and gave the little girl her first taste of sherry.

Once the war was over and Summer Fields 'mi' had returned to St Leonard's, John and GB were able to start building up a younger staff, beginning with the return of Pat Marston, Pat Savage and Jimmy Bell. GB could also settle down to enjoying cricket once more in the Parks, revelling in the glories of Donnelly.

1946. . . . C. B. Fry, as good a judge of cricket as there has ever been, said emphatically that not one of the left-handers of his day was Donnelly's superior: he might hesitate a little over Woolley and Clem Hill, but could any praise be higher than that? There was not a stroke of which Donnelly was not the master. His off- and straight drives were perhaps the most attractive, but in leg-hitting or in cutting he was almost equally great. He was a magnificent cover-point, a fair wicket-keeper and not to be despised as a bowler. Never have the Parks been fuller than 1946–7 and they filled up again when he appeared there for the last time in 1949. He was playing for the New Zealanders then, and the crowd applauded him all the way to the wicket.

(In the varsity match) Donnelly had to come in when the light was none too good and was forced to play a defensive innings after Sale left. Griffiths and Trapnell bowled well. Another of the Cambridge bowlers had an action which was something more than dubious. Asked about him after the match, Donnelly said, 'Oh yes, he threw all right. But you wouldn't want to no-ball such a friendly bowler!'

On Monday Donnelly got to work with the first ball sent down. The glory of his batting can hardly be described. In an hour and three quarters he made 113 out of 147 with no semblance of a chance. As usual, he employed all the strokes, his driving being magnificent. If ever there was a better century in the Varsity match it was R. E. Foster's (171 in 1900): those who saw both may dispute the matter if they will.

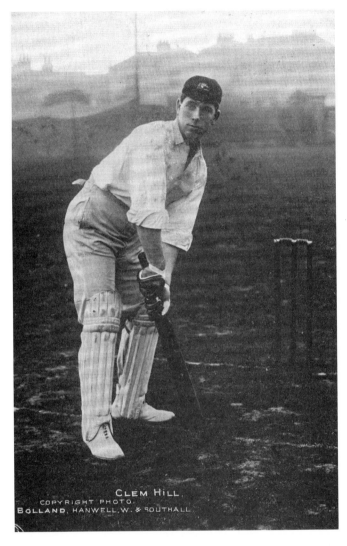

Clem Hill.

Notes:

1. We know from Straton-Ferrier's account in the previous chapter that this was not always true; but post-war he tended to be called simply GB by the boys (though not to his face). JFE seems to have been first Tark(y) and later Ticky.
2. Presumably these are Harry Altham, Martin Donnelly and GB; Donnelly had gone up to Worcester College in 1945.

School photograph 1948. The war is over, but few look anything approaching happy. The prize for the most miserable face might well be shared by JFE and GB, but there is strong competition immediately behind them in Willy Pryor and John Armstrong-Macdonnell. Behind them, beaming like a good deed in a naughty world, Larry Rawstorne actually does radiate happiness.

CHAPTER 8: MID-CENTURY BLUES

AFTER THE WAR, the school continued to be in debt, and was rather shabby. GB handed over the editorship of the magazine to Pat Savage in 1946.

> And here the Editor, as such, takes leave of his readers. After holding the position for sixteen years, he feels that he has by now committed all the errors of which an editor *can* be guilty and that it is time for somebody else to have a shot.

He continued to run Cottage, however, where he was soon joined by Pat Savage and Jimmy Bell. Despite having three men to run the lodge, it was left to the boys and Miss Morgan on Sunday evenings when there was a visiting preacher to entertain. There was dinner in the Front, which all resident bachelors attended. GB would see the boys through their washing and into bed, and would then walk across to the school, under the impression that they were unaware of being left to their own devices.

Those dinners in the Front were considered trying or amusing, depending on your viewpoint, the visiting preacher and how mischievous the younger masters were feeling. Jimmy Bell used to revel in 'pranks', such as putting a rubber worm into GB's glass of water – water being the only drink offered to accompany the meal. There was a glass of sherry beforehand, but nobody other than the preacher was offered a second glass. If the visitor came from nearby, GB would often fetch and return him in the Lanchester. On one occasion, he arrived at Pusey House to collect a well-known preacher and was kept waiting interminably. This inspired him to devise a couplet:

> Here I wait, and is he ready?
> No, of course he's not; it's Freddie!

He might well have said "Fleddie", for this particular clergyman suffered from the speech defect known as lambdacisation, which inserts l or substitutes it for other letters, especially r.[1] 'Fleddie' once preached a sermon on the three different Greek words for love: *philia, agape* and *'elloes'*!

And so to Monday morning. Miss Morgan is the first person up and about: white-haired, spruce, crisp in manner and with a Welsh twinkle, she runs a tight ship with exactly the right blend of respect and dominance. She wakes GB and brings him his cup of tea so that he has time to wash and dress before he calls the boys at ten past seven, by which time he has run them a cold bath. *"Surgite!"* he intones, and eighteen boys, clad only in white towels, spill out of the four dormitories and trot along to the bathroom. Here they shed the towels and immerse themselves one by one, GB supervising from the head end of the bath. The same water does for everybody; if you can time it right, you can get the wake to spill out of the top end of the bath, with a chance of wetting GB's ankles and shoes. He is not amused.

He finishes dressing while Miss Morgan calls Jimmy Bell and Pat Savage, and then he goes over to the school, probably in the company of one or two boys. It is a peaceful school at this hour, with the smell of newly lit, lukewarm coal fires in winter, and the murmur of boys gradually accustoming themselves to the day. This is a period when GB socialises, going from room to room, seeing that Fifth Form are looking at their Greek grammars (which they will also take into breakfast), commenting on something in the day's paper, preferably some sporting news, teasing small boys – the period that has been feelingly described as 'funny jokes in Greek before breakfast'.

The bell goes. It is time for line-up, Lower School in their own room, the others in the corridors. When they are all marshalled and the silence bell has gone, GB leads the procession from the lobby up to the dining room, along the tiled passage under its glass roof, his grey-flannelled legs striding out, his marionette-like arms sketching an imaginary cricket shot. Once the school is assembled at the tables, he says, "We will have grace. Say grace," and a prefect declaims, *"Benedic nobis, Domine Deus . . . "* Breakfast is a comparatively quiet meal; after a quarter of an hour, GB or JFE, who will by now have appeared, pings the bell and says, "You may read when you've finished." Greek grammars appear once more, together with library books and morning papers: there is an air of both academe and a gentlemen's club.

After breakfast there is Bible-reading for the whole school in New Room: the boys sit round the room as a chapter of the Bible, usually the New Testament, is read, each boy taking a verse in turn. GB does not appear at this; it is taken by Lysaght or JFE. If JFE is not there, he will probably be in the Study with GB, conning the morning's post. Then it is time for lessons – three forty-minute periods before break. At least one of these will be Fifth Form, either in Fifth Form Room or in French Room; in each case the boys sit around a long table, and answer questions in order: grammar, vocabulary or *Borva Notes.*

These are a set of points in classical languages to be learnt, distinguished or parsed. Originally created by Dr Williams when he was inhabiting Borva, the house he built in 1881 on the Banbury Road, they have been subsequently adapted by 'Bear' Alington and then GB himself. GB has mixed feelings about the original:

> Borva Notes caused a lot of trouble. The Doctor had never believed in taking chances, and in this work he had collected all the grammatical questions which might conceivably be asked by any examiner. There were many words of which I had (and have) never heard; but there was also tremendous attention to detail,

and any boy who really knew his Borva Notes was extremely well-equipped. In later years, when the supply of books ran out, I produced an amended version (*A Classical Notebook*, 1951) which omitted much that was unnecessary but adhered closely to the main principles.

Second lesson may well be Middle Fourth, starting Greek. They are taught at a long trestle table in the Gym. GB either sits at one end, again firing questions or calling up boys in turn to have their exercises corrected, or stands at the blackboard and easel writing with the scratchy chalk in his spidery hand. A colleague recalls, "that apparently elastic left arm, both in the squash court and across the blackboard; I think he was one of the most left-sided of all lefties (in everything except batting and politics!). I never saw him kick a football with his right foot and, though I am sure he could catch with his right hand, I don't recall his doing so." Incidentally, he caned with his left hand, back-hand, much as one would play a cut in cricket.

One of the features of Summer Fields is a long morning break. In summer this will mean fielding practice with the Under-10s, but in winter terms GB is at leisure, having passed on the soccer to Harold Hartley. Often both his Classics forms will have another lesson with him after break, and in this case he sometimes takes then simultaneously in Fifth Form Room, skilfully alternating oral with written work for each group and somehow managing to answer every question when somebody gets stuck. Lunch is taken *à deux* at Top Table with JFE, waited upon by the ghostly Gardner. The two headmasters talk in a desultory fashion ("mainly shop," as GB puts it), GB chews each mouthful twenty-three times according to legend, and at the end of the meal, after the second post is given out, JFE reads out the sides for the afternoon games for the entire school: "First game Red: . . . " His enunciation is not impeccable, and it is sometimes hard to hear which side one is on; there is fun, too, if the school contains a boy called White and he's playing for the Reds. After lunch, if GB isn't taking games (and he usually is), he goes for a brisk walk down the farm fields, through the allotments, up the Marston Ferry Road and so back by the Banbury Road. Then there is correcting to be done, thoroughly but with no time wasted, and not in red ink but in his Eversharp silver propelling pencil.

Tea for the masters is in the drawing room, while the boys have a slice of bread-and-jam (no butter) at a trolley in the kitchen passage. There are two more lessons before supper, chapel or prayers, and then prep – unless it is a Saturday, when there is no prep and GB will take Black Book after supper while the majority are watching the film show projected by Eric Bowtell in New Room. On an ordinary evening, GB will have an early supper and prepare to 'do' Cottage at 8.30; but very occasionally he has an evening off, and then there may be an excursion to the theatre or a dinner party. The cricket writer E. W. Swanton, who was living at Pusey House after the war, remembers taking Martin Donnelly up to Summer Fields for dinner with JFE and GB. "They kept a very good table and, as it was a time of acute rationing, I could not help wondering if we were taking the food out of the boys' mouths."

Cottage are washed, bathed, tucked into bed with a good book and turned out by 9.20. Then any more correcting can be done, or possibly some reading or listening to the wireless. GB was, in the opinion of Jimmy Bell, one of the best-read people that he knew. One wonders how he found time to read much during term, and also how he contrived to see a bit of every match that was played at the Parks between 1920 and 1960. Perhaps that is just another GB myth. Anyway, the day certainly ends with one. At 10.07 exactly, he goes up to bed. If he cannot sleep, he recites the *Iliad* or the *Odyssey*, both of which he knows by heart, taking up at the line where he last went to sleep:

Τὸν δ᾽ ἀπαμειβόμενος προσέφη πολύμητις ᾽Οδυσσεύς . . .

To be in Cottage under GB, Pat Savage and Jimmy Bell was stimulating. As you see, GB began the day with Latin and ended it with Greek, but there was a lot more to it than an aura of classical culture. Pat and Jimmy were inveterate book-lovers and theatregoers, making frequent sorties into Oxford, to Blackwell's in the afternoon and the New Theatre or the Playhouse in the evening. They were also avid pranksters, who respected GB as something of a father figure but enjoyed the occasional joke at his expense. On one occasion, however, the laugh was on them, as Pat relates:

> Jimmy and I were in theory supposed to deputise for GB, but he hardly ever went away, or even out. He had a regular, rigid routine last thing at night: up to bed at 10.07, then Thucydides or some other Greek author until lights-out at perhaps 10.30. One evening Jimmy and I were feeling extremely hungry – after School tea at 6 o'clock – so we decided to go round to the Fish & Chip shop at 10. When we came back, we saw that, surprisingly, the lights were still on in GB's study. It was unthinkable that we should confront him bearing these plebeian foodstuffs. So we walked round the block again. Again still on. Again. (It is amazing that we, who had recently been a major and a captain in the army, should be so in awe of GB!) Still on. Eventually, as the food became colder and clammier, I said, "There's only one thing to do. You put these in the kitchen. I shall go and say good-night to him." I knocked respectfully on the door of the study. No answer. I went in. It was just that he had gone to bed, but forgotten to turn the lights out.

PMBS, as has already been said, liked and admired GB, but found him an interesting, not to say amazing, phenomenon.

> GB had some likes and dislikes that didn't always seem consistent with his normally conservative attitudes. He ate strawberry jam at breakfast instead of marmalade, and there were some quite innocuous things that were anathema to him, such as onions, nutmeg and cats. It was a special mark of his appreciation that he allowed Miss Morgan to keep a cat at Cottage.
>
> He wore a faded sports-jacket and grey flannel 'bags' almost all the time – even on formal occasions when others were wearing suits. He was reputed to have refused an invitation from the Freybergs to dine at Windsor Castle, when he was with the scholars at Eton, because he would have had to wear a suit. It was a surprise and a shock to Jimmy and me, when we were gurgling with laughter as we told him that we had just discovered that a colleague didn't wear pants, that GB said in the curious flat, uninflected tone that he adopted when he was put out, 'I wear no pants.'

Pat Savage (right), pictured here with John Evans and Charles Marnham at the school's Centenary Sherry Party.

Charles Hossell came onto the staff at Summer Fields when 'Liz' Lysaght became ill, and he attributes his appointment to GB, who had got to know him at St Edward's.

I was demobbed in February 1948 and at a loose end before returning to Trinity, when I had a phone call from GB asking me if I would like to help out for the Summer Term. I set out post-haste and was interviewed by GB, who was prepared to accept my Maths without question, and my Latin with some scepticism; but, when I responded to his enquiry into my Greek by saying that I found the alphabet widely used in Maths, he exploded with 'prostitution of a noble language.'

My temporary appointment became more permanent when GB asked me if I could help with Fifth Form Maths while Liz was out of action. In return, I came to live in the school rather than digs in North Oxford, and, with some adjusting of the timetable around my tutorials, my time at Summer Fields began. I owe much to GB from what I gained between meeting him in 1943 at Teddies and 1956, when I joined ICI. To my youthful eyes at Teddies, he was an awesomely friendly man, whose surprising shafts of wit (usually re cricket) generated a shaking of the shoulders and created quite a different picture from his normally austere persona. He even came to accept that the times were changing and that excellence in Classics was no longer the sole key to the door. He was a fund of information and very self-controlled; a rare word of praise was to be treasured. I also treasure an invitation to watch his beloved Sussex at Hove at the end of the Summer Term. To witness the journey from his deckchair by the sightscreen to the pavilion at the lunch interval was to see a royal progress.

This cordial picture is matched by a story from Mike Gover, who was later to become headmaster at the Dragon School, the famous rival school down the Banbury Road. But he was only a junior master when, in the early 1950s, GB rang up Joc Lynam and told him that Harold Clayton was going up to the test match at Lord's and would be happy to give anyone from the Dragon School a lift. Mike jumped at the opportunity and reckons that Harold must have delivered them to the Grace Gate in record time in those days before motorways; most of the journey had been spent on two wheels and in a jellified state.

Mike Gover.

They were met by GB, who immediately restored their spirits with another kind of spirit in generous measures and invited them to lunch in the interval. In the restaurant, GB was the perfect host. Delicious salmon was matched by delicious wine, and the company was regaled with tales of cricketing personalities and the Sussex Martlets, which kept them spellbound. After such friendly generosity, Mike even enjoyed the trip back and was delivered in one piece, somewhat to his surprise, to the Dragon School, no longer trembling.

Some days later, he met GB coming out of the Parks as he went in and was amazed to receive absolutely no response to his greeting.

> Had I forgotten to write a thank-you letter? Or had GB got to the age, which I certainly have now, when memory becomes non-existent concerning people's names and recent happenings, while easily remembering what happened fifty years ago?" GB the mystery.

Derek Henderson was at St Edward's at the same time as Charles Hossell and he was captain of the XI in 1944. He asked GB to umpire some school matches:

> an invitation he accepted with boyish enthusiasm; he did the job superbly. He always sat at the umpires' table at lunch and was a real professional at the job.
>
> Then I was in the Navy, and had no further contact until 1947. I had been to see Henry Kendall to ask his help in getting into Oxford. As this was not to happen until October, Henry rang John Evans to ask whether he needed any temporary help for the summer term. The answer was 'No,' but that evening I was rung at home by GB and told to report at once!

I loved my time at Summer Fields: I worked hard, did duty twice a week and took the 2nd XI. But, horror of horrors, I taught in the Gym at the far end, with GB at the other. He was taking the scholars: I was teaching French, of which I knew little and managed to keep one day ahead of the boys. I learnt through experience to teach when he taught and be silent when he was silent. They were difficult times.

He had a mark book going back years. His forms were given the same proses and unseens year by year. From his mark book he could forecast with amazing accuracy the results of his scholars-to-be. The one I remember was Mortimer, son of the Bishop of Exeter. He just knew he would be No. 1 at Eton, and he was.[2]

In the holidays he took me to Brighton to play for the Sussex Martlets against the Old Brightonians. We stayed at the Ship Hotel and lived in style. Jimmy Bell came as well, and GB was a wonderfully generous host: we were not allowed to pay for anything.

Up at Trinity, I shared rooms with Micky Jones (later bursar of Radley and chairman of the Summer Fields Governors) and in '47, '48 and '49 we had a 'GB evening'. I used to go back to SF after the end of the university term, but, thank goodness, I did not teach in the Gym!

And then, alas, came the end of our friendship. I let him down and he never forgave me. I was in the University XI in 1950. He had asked me to play for his XI against North Oxford, and I had accepted. The game was to take place on a Thursday. Late on Wednesday evening, Chris Winn, secretary of O.U.C.C., came to my room and told me I was needed to play for the Free Foresters against the University on the next day. I could not say no. I wrote a note to GB and took it up to Cottage; I knew it was no good trying to see him; he always went to bed early. He never spoke to me again.

In the years after the war, the nucleus of an excellent permanent staff arrived, as well as the three returning, Marston, Savage and Bell, who taught until 1970, 1975 and 1978 respectively – though JLB continued to teach part-time until 1985. GB was also instrumental in engaging for brief periods keen young sportsmen, initially from Teddies, such as Hossell, Henderson and Mike Womersley; more regularly from the Sussex Martlets, as Simon Starkey (who was also a Reptonian), David Mordaunt, Chris Saunders and Chris Snell; or from Oxford, such as Fran Prichard and Andrew Corran. Chris Snell also had the connection that his father, Edward, had been a Summer Fields master with GB in the late 1920s. A large proportion of these young men became headmasters in the fullness of time.

GB was highly active on the committee of the Sussex Martlets throughout this period. In 1946, he had been elected a vice-president 'in recognition of his services to the Club', and he was chosen as one of the match managers from 1948 onwards. In November 1950, the committee decided to elect him as president for the ensuing three years; but he in fact held the office for the rest of his life.

The situation of the Junior Martlets was also discussed, and it was suggested that it might be well to ask Geoffrey Bolton his views on the matter and as to whether he would undertake the organization of the Junior Martlets next year by himself or in collaboration with W. O'Byrne.

David Mordaunt and Chris Saunders, Sussex Martlets, who taught at Summer Fields. David went on to be a housemaster at Wellington and played for Berkshire; Chris played for both Oxford and Cambridge and was headmaster of Eastbourne and then Lancing.

Another Martlet, Chris Snell, who followed his father, Edward, as both a master at Summer Fields and then headmaster of Mowden School in Hove.

Nothing apparently came of this: it would have been hard for him to make all the arrangements from Oxford.

Another ex-Martlet GB introduced to the school was David Sheppard, whom he invited down to preach at evensong and to talk to some of the boys afterwards. Sheppard was at that time already an England cricketer and preparing to take holy orders; he was involved also with a group called VPSC (Varsity and Public Schools Camps), which organised holiday house parties with evangelistic overtones. Sheppard did some proselytising at Summer Fields, presumably with GB's knowledge and approval.

Though Summer Fields' ship of state was apparently well manned and on an even keel, all was not entirely well. As has been indicated, the strain had begun to tell upon John Evans, who had already had one breakdown in 1943, and inevitably this put a strain upon GB, who had to cope while pretending that life was continuing as normal. The contrast between the two men is well presented by Ralph Hulbert, who was a new boy at the school in 1948.

> My parents sent me to Summer Fields because it was then considered in polite society that there were only two proper prep schools – SF if the boy was bright, Ludgrove if he was not. My father, a consultant neurologist, quickly came to the conclusion that John Evans was off balance and heading for a nervous breakdown (inter alia, because of the titles in his bookcase). But he concluded that the school was in fact run by GB, whom he did not think to be at all mad. He used to recount how the fresh new parents on Sports Days etc. would rush up to JFE asking, 'So how is little Johnny doing?' and duly being told, 'Wonderfully well,' whereas the old hands went to GB to be told, 'Well, all right, if I keep on kicking him.'

A corollary to that is remembered by Jonathan Alexander, a promising pupil who was thoroughly shaken when GB told his parents that he was rather a spoilt little boy who did not work hard enough. He worked much harder after that and in due course won a scholarship to Radley.

> GB was considered a sort of ogre [Ralph continues], but I never found that; insofar as I had to deal with him, I liked him and have happy memories (this was certainly not so of all the staff). He introduced me to squash and must have played with me on a number of occasions. I felt privileged to have so much of his time, and look back on it with considerable affection, not least because squash became my main game in my 20s and 30s.
>
> I remember once the boy who said grace getting the giggles and totally botching it up. We waited in mild trepidation to see what GB would do. In fact, when the boy finished, all he said was, 'Have a second helping.'

This presents GB in a complimentary light, but there is no doubt that, as Ralph says, to some he was an ogre. Peter Davies has already been mentioned and Toby Eady, an exact contemporary, also comes into this category.

> The kindest words that I have for GB are that it was unfortunate that he taught me at the end of his career, and when he played cricket, he was a different man, both his body language and enthusiasm. In truth GB terrorised me. Jimmy Bell

taught me and, if I had had him throughout my time at SF, then I would have a very different view of it as a school: he was a teacher, not an enforcer of knowledge.

When I went up to Oxford, I heard through the grapevine that there was a party for Old Boys. I wasn't invited my first year; and, when I went my second year because of Jimmy Bell, GB graciously said he was surprised to see me, as he never thought I would get to Oxford.

But, if there were bêtes noires, there were also the favoured and the favourites. Two boys (future Reptonians living in Sussex), who arrived the same term as Hulbert and Eady would every day at the beginning of break don their boots and sweaters and go to a point at the edge of the Masters' Lawn opposite the Study windows. As soon as GB saw them, he would drop everything and set out to join them for a walk around the fields.

According to PMBS:

> John and GB didn't really get on. It took me some time to realise this. It appeared on the surface to be such a splendid partnership – and, of course, from the School's point of view it was. They complemented each other perfectly. John did the drudgery in the Study, presiding over everything officially as HM – at Prizegivings, Masters' Meetings, in Chapel – and saw the parents, whether he liked them or not. This left GB free to deal with what he was superbly good at – teaching Fifth Form, running Cottage, bowling in the nets and refereeing matches. He also took the Black Book on Saturdays, which relieved John of some of the unpleasantness of beating boys. It ought to have been an admirable arrangement, but they each slightly *envied* the other, I think. It was only over the school and its welfare that their minds met. Otherwise, they were like a hot and a cold tap, whose water mixes beautifully in the bath; but the taps don't meet.

In the school photographs of the 1950s, the strain shows clearly in the faces of both headmasters. John Evans broke down in January 1953; as the school descended into a double epidemic and the matron walked out, he was hauled off to the Acland Nursing Home, where he was told that he must take six months' rest. 'This term began as badly as possible and then got worse,' as the magazine concisely puts it. But GB weathered the storms: at least Jimmy Bell had taken on Fifth Form in September, so he no longer had that to worry about. And *ex amaro surrexit aliquid boni*; the departure of one matron was followed by the arrival of Nancy Lovett, who was a tower of strength in years to come.

But, though JFE was back and apparently restored to health in September, it was clearly time to look to the future. When the final 'crack' did come, who would succeed, and how? As GB says:

> For some time it had been plain that the future of the School was precarious. We were both bachelors and heirless: whom were we likely to find ready and able to take on not only the School but the mortgage which we had incurred in buying out the Williams-Alington interest?

Clearly we had to become a Trust with a Board of Governors who would ensure that the School would carry on. With much care we chose our Governors and, after protracted legal negotiations, we finally became the Summer Fields [School] Trust Ltd in September 1955. That was virtually John's last act as Headmaster. In the Easter and Summer terms of 1956 he became less and less fit. He survived the gruelling first day of the September term, but fell seriously ill after the week-end. [In those days the school reassembled on Fridays.] It was plain that he would never again be able to do the job, and on October 15th the Governors appointed me in his stead.

This was a sad ending to a career which had started in 1914 and to 17 years of headmastership in particularly difficult circumstances. It is true to say that Summer Fields was the only mundane interest in John's life. He gave everything that he had to the School, and I feel that in retirement he must have been conscious of work well done. I shall not pretend that in our long association we always saw eye to eye, nor will I deny that he could be very difficult to work with; but of his single-minded devotion there can be no question. I do not think that, when things were going wrong in the 1930s, either of us ever doubted that the luck would turn; he, more than anybody, was responsible for the fact that it did.

This is a loyal tribute, perhaps more notable for its charity than its accuracy. PMBS felt that GB had a sense of having missed his moment when John returned from his 1953 collapse.

It was particularly hard for him, because John grew more and more difficult and exhausting for everyone else as he himself became more exhausted. When he finally left in 1956 – horizontally, in an ambulance – , poor GB had to pick up the bits. By then he was far too weary and worn out to enjoy what he had so long wanted and waited for. He only survived as HM for four years and didn't appear to like it much.

GB with his boyhood hero C. B. Fry at Martlets Jubilee Dinner, 1955.

Notes:

1. And this is incidentally said to have given the name of Bristol its form, that being the way in which its inhabitants pronounced Bristowe!
2. In fact, Mark Mortimer narrowly missed first scholarship: he was second on the Roll, as was his brother Edward in 1956. But they were both undoubtedly 'top scholars' in the general sense.

The school photograph, 1956, with both headmasters showing signs of strain.

CHAPTER 9: HEADMASTER

THE SECOND HALF of 1956 was momentous for Summer Fields, as there was a change of leader both in the country and in the school. Harold Macmillan, who had been a boy at Summer Fields, 1903–6, became prime minister; and Geoffrey Bolton became headmaster. The school magazine for December 1956:

> In schools less firmly founded a change of headmasters might be observed with uneasiness. We are more than usually fortunate in having as Mr Evans's successor Mr Bolton, who has earned everyone's confidence and respect as a partner for twenty-seven years and has already had a reassuring amount of successful practice in running most branches of school activity at some time or other.

Though some might have expected the promotion of one of the two Old Summerfieldians on the staff, Pat Marston or Jimmy Bell, the choice of Patrick Savage as GB's assistant headmaster was imaginative and successful. He was twenty-three years younger than GB, creative and inventive and, though staunchly conservative, good at devising ways of making the school run more smoothly. Tactfully and discreetly, he nudged GB into introducing various changes. They were never close to each other, both being to some extent shy and having few interests in common – but they certainly shared a deep love of Summer Fields, and so the partnership, though not a 'marriage of true minds', was efficient and productive and gave PMBS an excellent 'running-in' period for his own important and longer headmastership.

He did not find it entirely easy, though.

> I really knew less of what was going on than I had before. GB didn't confide in me much, and it was difficult dealing with the Governors because of that. My appointment did not imply any 'right of succession', but it was easy to see where all this might be leading. It was not what I had planned or hoped for; but there had been talk of 'somebody from outside'; so I accepted.

Immediate changes included the incorporation of Bible-reading into morning prayers, the institution of a Chapel Fund, the buying of new prayer books and some modification of the long Sunday services. The hand of PMBS is clearly discernible here, but GB, the agnostic, must surely have approved of such simplification. JFE had always read the lesson himself at every service; GB did not continue the custom, but introduced a welcome variety of voice with the 'master on duty'.

Prefects were given more power and more privileges, with the restoration of the Prefects' Book and the Prefects' Dinner. JFE had tended simply to let the prefects get on with things – which had laid the system open to abuse – but the new team talked to them more and expected more of them. They were not disappointed. One of GB's later head prefects was Roderick Dunnett:

> It was on the last day of the summer term of 1959 that GB called me to his study to inform me that I would be Head Prefect for the following year. He perhaps sensed that I was diffident by nature and would make a mark more by example than by force of personality. He said that his door would always be open and that he would support me and Peter Kay, who was made my deputy. I was very proud of the honour and could not sleep that night. At the end of my two terms as Head Prefect I went for the summer term to take up my scholarship at Eton. GB wrote to thank me for having set a good example.
>
> GB was certainly instrumental in my going to Eton. My parents had had at first no such idea. The tradition that GB took the scholarship candidates to Eton is well-known. I found his manner and concern greatly aided our calmness and readiness. The eveningtime P. G. Wodehouse stories in a private sitting-room at the hotel are a happy memory. Another aspect of that tradition was the encounter outside School Hall of recent OSS, who came to pay their respects and talk excitedly of life in the bigger school.

Owing to a sudden departure from the staff, GB had also had to take on the cricket in 1956.

> There could hardly have been a worse moment for me personally, but for the moment there was no-one else. Of course I loved every minute of it, exhausting as it was.

It was as well that there was a good supply of keen young cricketing masters to assist him, for his age (he was now sixty-three) and the other demands upon him made him less than patient with the shortcomings of his players. GB stuck to the principle that the batting and bowling could to some extent look after themselves, but that you must field well. He rammed this home assiduously. David Calvert-Smith, one of the school's finest all-round sporting luminaries, on one occasion failed to stop a stinger in fielding practice and was thereafter considered to have a 'yellow streak' – a slur which no amount of subsequent heroics fully expunged.

Christopher Poole, captain of the 1959 XI, was once found distraught with tears behind the pavilion, crying, "I hate GB! I hate GB!" The cause has been lost in history, but it was probably a lack of tact. For instance, in those days, when the 1st XI played the staff in the end-of-term 'Broomstick Match', 2nd XI boys umpired. They did not, of course, always get it right; but it was a good-humoured occasion and questionable decisions were accepted with a good grace. This year, a young master was rapped on the pad, the XI appealed, the umpire raised his finger and the master walked – only to meet GB striding from the pavilion and proclaiming, "Go back! Nonsense, Simon, it wasn't out."

Embarrassment for the master, public humiliation for the boy umpire: not the best way to encourage young cricketers.

He continued to be generous, though, with both praise and criticism in writing up a season: here is part of the 1957 review:

We had expected to have a weak team this year, but the forecast was that, though we should not make many runs, the bowling would be adequate. This turned out to be over-optimistic! Letts only once bowled really well; for some reason he had lost all length and direction. Broke ma was equally disappointing; and only Daniels could be regarded as a dangerous bowler.

The batting was much as expected. Kaplowitch played one great innings and two very useful ones. Faber was clearly the best batsman, but made only one good score, frequently giving his wicket away just when he looked set. Burnett-Hitchcock and Rodgers hit hard at times; Calvert-Smith often looked good, but could not cope with a half-volley! The others from whom runs were expected – Letts, Daniels and Poole ma – invariably committed suicide, often just as they were getting going.

The fielding was often good and never became ragged. Daniels was outstandingly good and Faber very reliable. Rodgers, Asquith ma and Letts were usually competent.

A weak team? Anyone who looks at the photograph of the Eton XI for 1962 will find that it includes Daniels, Calvert-Smith and Faber – all of whom stayed on in 1958's "best cricket season for many years" – and Letts was twelfth man.

Cricket XI, 1958: the best 1st XI ever? (Standing) Hugh Keep, Andrew Thompson, Roderick Macpherson, Robert Tabor; (seated) Christopher Poole, Michael Faber, Rupert Daniels, David Calvert-Smith, Robin Broke; (on the ground) David Wilson and Richard Smith.

There is a halo over that side in my memory, as there is over the 1936 soccer side. We were unbeaten by any prep school (Bradfield Under-14 alone defeated us), but we had one incredibly close match. Put in to bat by Horris Hill (of all people) on their ground, we declared at 135 for 7. Thanks to superb bowling and fielding we had six of them out for 26 with an hour to go. In despair their two batsmen (one of them a really fine player) began to hit. Only one catch was dropped, but the ground fielding went to pieces, save for a brilliant run-out which saved us in the last over, and the final score was:

Summer Fields 135 for 7 dec.
Horris Hill 135 for 7.

Meanwhile, at Summer Fields, our 2nd XI was defeating theirs by 1 run.

This same term arrived at Summer Fields a diminutive figure, Michael Faber's younger brother Mark, who made his way straight into the Under-10 team. He was very much smiled upon by GB, who referred to him as the Little Man. Small in stature indeed he was, but a great cricketer who would one day play for Sussex. The arrival of Duncan Williams and David Mordaunt on the teaching staff gradually relieved GB of the onerous duties of first game.

He also at this period was holding his third term of office as president of the Sussex Martlets. A letter from L. V. Donne to Eddie Harrison, secretary of the Sussex Martlets, 13th August 1956:

On the agenda there is of course Item No. 5: 'Nomination of President for 1957–59.' Personally, if Geoffrey Bolton will take it on, I am sure it would be a good thing to elect him for a further three years. He is one of the few Presidents who give any sort of attention to the job and he is of course 100%.

This testifies that GB showed equal commitment to the Sussex Martlets as to Summer Fields.

In his four years as headmaster, the worst crisis that GB had to cope with was the arrest of a member of staff for an offence in an Oxford lavatory. The timing of this was cruel: at the end of the Lent term, just before he was about to go off on a long-awaited tour of Greece with Jonathan Roberts. GB felt that he must stay at school and face the press and any possible repercussions; so he sent PMBS off on the Greek trip and stayed behind. In the event, there was minimal press coverage and the matter settled down.

The most important innovation of GB's short term as headmaster was the opening of an Appeal Fund. This was a step in the right direction, as the school's finances had been in a woeful state since the 1930s. An Endowment Appeal Dinner was held at Claridge's in November 1957 and it was attended by the Prime Minister (despite a heavy cold) and other distinguished OSS. The Bishop of Exeter, as chairman of the governors, was in the chair, and other speeches were made by the Prime Minister and GB.

The Headmaster . . . compared his present situation with a nightmare that he had once had, in which he was touched on the shoulder at Lords and told, 'Sutcliffe is waiting for you.' He felt like that now. 'Who is that man?' the diners would be saying, 'he is neither Maclaren, nor Williams, nor Alington.' He could only plead that there was one of the fifth generation of the Founders' family [Nichol Marston] teaching in the School today. He said that he had not had the honour of teaching the Prime Minister himself, but that he had had the distinction of having under him two members of Her Majesty's Government, John Acheson (the Earl of Gosford) and Julian Amery; the former he had tried to teach, the latter invariably tried to teach him! He then congratulated G. O. Allen (Chairman of the Test selectors) on gathering a side who could win a Test Match in three days – the correct time for a Test Match – and added that the School had achieved a notable hat-trick in the last three Governors-General of New Zealand, General Freyberg, General Willoughby Norrie, and Lord Cobham. Greatly encouraged by the appointment of the Prime Minister, the School had done very well recently in its scholastic achievements and this year had a 100 per cent scholarship record. In conclusion, he asked all OSS to visit the School as often as possible and see for themselves.

This invitation was taken up the following summer by the Prime Minister himself, who came to revisit the school on 25th June after attending the Vice Chancellor's Garden Party. Unfortunately, the weather was distinctly wet, but it relented enough for everyone to be able to watch Macmillan plant a commemorative tulip tree on the Masters' Lawn. Accompanied by Lady Dorothy Macmillan, he then made a thorough tour of the school and apparently had no difficulty in locating his old desk in New Room. Little more than a year later, he would not have been able to do so as, in a major and necessary refurbishment, the old six-seater desks, their lids criss-crossed with carved names and ink-runs, were removed and replaced by modern flat-topped ones. GB was said to have wept at their departure.

New Room, with the old six-seater desks.

135

Visit of the Prime Minister, Harold Macmillan.
The school lined the passages as GB escorted Macmillan
down to the 'old' lobby, which was to undergo a transformation in 1960.

He had by now been at Summer Fields for almost forty years and made good use of all the memories and school lore that he had willingly acquired over that time. For the diamond jubilee of the magazine (the last and most splendid of PMBS's editorship), he contributed a set of memoirs called 'Five Wise Men': Crofts, 'Bam' Evans, Smyth, Penny and Case. In subsequent issues, he found himself again in the role of obituarist (whose subject, in a school magazine, may be either the dead or the retired living): he wrote appreciations of Miss Hill mi; Gill Alington (Bobs' wife); the faithful Hill, backbone of the maintenance department for more than fifty years; and L. A. G. Strong.

His eulogistic account of Hill omits a paragraph which he did include in his essay on 'The Leagues' in *A Century of Summer Fields*:

> At the end of each term the winning league and its leaders had their names inscribed on a panel in New Room . . . When the panels in New Room were filled up, others were made in the dining-room. I suggested this and Hill said, "What a good idea." I felt exactly as I did when, long years ago, Tom Hayward had said, 'Well bowled, sir,' at a net in the Parks. GB the hero-worshipper.

Of Strong he wrote:

> Not only was he a fine teacher; he was instinctively sympathetic by nature and was a man of deep understanding . . . When he came back to see us, he was at home with the boys at once. His criticisms of their poetry reading were generous and sympathetic. He knew too which stories would give them most pleasure. He was a devotee of Wodehouse, but the lack of dialect in, say, the Jeeves stories, would have handicapped him. He was most at home with his dearly loved W. W. Jacobs and with any story which could use a strong Irish accent.
> As would be expected of a 'fan' of Jacobs, Leonard loved the simple joke. Long ago it was customary for a boy who had done well at something to say, "Sweat by me!" Leonard told an eight-year-old in one of his forms that 'sweat' was a coarse word and that he should always say, 'perspiration.' Which the child accordingly did, to the delight of all who heard him. He had, too, a wicked raise of one eyebrow with which he could (and did) drive one into agonies of suppressed laughter at moments when laughter was wildly out of place. GB the giggler again.

With two bachelor headmasters, it might be felt that the school was drily Spartan, though of course Nancy Lovett, the matron, made an excellent mother-substitute for those who were ill. Perdita Marston, the founders' great-granddaughter, came most suitably into such a role for the small boys, to whom she would read on Sundays and on whom she would keep a maternal eye at other times. A further feminine influence was the introduction of an annual dance with Greycotes, the girls' school "down the road", which gave more point to the Thursday afternoon dancing lessons in the dining room.

Summer 1959 was a glorious, golden one with all the traditional Summer Fields events taking place in blazing sunshine, a good crop of scholarships and a general election in which seven Old Summerfieldians and eight Summerfieldian fathers were successful (all Conservatives, of course!). God seemed to be very much in his heaven and all right with the world. But within a year the blow fell, as Pat Savage relates.

> GB actually, but not noticeably, was becoming increasingly ill; but it so happened that, at the crucial moment in 1960 we had a charming but diffident school doctor, who felt that his hand needed to be strengthened for GB to be told that, in the state of his heart, chest and lungs, he must not spend another winter at the School. So the Regius Professor of Medicine was brought in to examine him and pronounce the dire verdict. It was an appalling blow for him, and – as he said in his memoirs – he didn't (couldn't?) really believe it.

* * * * *

> I had hoped to stay as Headmaster till 1964 and retire after the Centenary celebrations. *Dis aliter visum.* When the doctors told me that I had had enough, I was reluctant to believe them – I'm not sure that I did (or do) believe them – but I felt that in fairness to the School, to the Governors and to my successors I *had* to believe them. So, after a shorter tenure than that of any previous Headmaster, I resigned from an office which had certainly been arduous but which, for the most part, I had thoroughly enjoyed.

At his own request, his final term and departure were markedly low-key. He hated farewells and feared that any big occasion might prove too much for him. Indeed, he was overcome in Prizegiving and had to leave it to PMBS. Richard Porthouse, a colleague with a penchant for romanticising, maintained that he and Duncan Williams took GB out for a farewell drink. In the car on the return journey, GB spoke disparagingly of Lonnie Donegan's song, 'My Old Man's a Dustman', going so far as to sing the original music-hall version:

> My old man's a fireman: he wears a fireman's hat;
> He wears a fireman's trousers – what d'you think of that?

He left at the end of term, wanting no fuss, so some sandwiches and a Thermos of coffee were left by his bedside, and he drove off to Sussex at 4.30 a.m. He did not drink the coffee, because, as he later admitted, he could not unscrew the Thermos.

GB lining up the Leagues for tea at his last Hay Feast.

Summer Fields Cricket 1st XI, 1961.

*(Standing) Martin Dyer, Rupert Parsons, David Roberts, Colin Middleton;
(seated) Nicholas Beer, Dennis Tabor, Peter Lowndes, George Chamier, Gilbert Chalk;
(on the ground) Mark Faber, Robin Grewal.*

"When GB left, it was the only headmaster's departure at which I wept." –
long-serving master at Summer Fields.

Danny, Hurstpierpoint.

CHAPTER 10: RETIREMENT

A MILE SOUTH OF HURSTPIERPOINT is a beautiful Elizabethan country house by the unusual name of Danny. It was bought in 1956 by the Country Houses Association, which had recently been formed to provide 'suitable accommodation for retired gentlefolk'. It seemed an ideal retirement place for GB, in the heart of his beloved Sussex, within easy reach of Hove and county cricket.

He found plenty to occupy him. He was preparing to write the history of Oxford University cricket. He went in to Hove regularly to do some part-time teaching at Mowden for Edward Snell, whose son Chris had meanwhile just started as a young master at Summer Fields – which Edward himself had done in 1928. Parties from the two schools, including GB, met for the varsity football match at Wembley in December. The new edition of the *Summer Fields Register*, expanded from GB's 1929 edition, was produced by Harold Clayton and published early in 1961. GB revisited the school twice in March, once on the 3rd, when he asked for a half-holiday, and again a fortnight later accompanied by George Cox, the Sussex cricketer, to "give the cricketers an early look at the ball"– memories of fielding practices on fine days at the end of so many Lent terms.

In 1961, the copyright for the Gilbert and Sullivan operas ran out. Hitherto, no professional company other than the D'Oyly Carte Opera Company had been allowed to perform them; but now the expectation was that the floodgates would be opened and, as in America and Germany, there would be jazz, swing and even rock versions of *The Mikado*. GB was taken to see the new Sadler's Wells production of *Iolanthe* at Stratford. He was not too upset by the (fairly uncontroversial) novelties which were introduced, but in his heart he remained firmly pro-D'Oyly Carte and the Lytton tradition.

That year the *Daily Telegraph* published advance notice of his OUCC opus.

Despite the great mass of cricket literature, the history of Oxford cricket has never been written. I hear – with some envy – from Geoffrey Bolton that, having recently retired from the headmastership of Summer Fields, he is now tackling the job.

No-one could be better qualified, for I suppose there is not a cricketer who has played for Oxford in half a century he has not known and watched . . . Mention of Mr Bolton will recall him to innumerable Oxford cricketers. With his very slow left-arm bowling he was a prolific undergraduate wicket-taker in April – most of them stumped off the pads of R. S. Thompson, ex-Sherborne, now headmaster of Bloxham.

In a letter to the same Stanley Thompson dated 16th February 1962, GB thanks him for promising to get the book and goes on to say that it:

has been great fun to do. I could have done one twice the size, and originally I had hoped for a number of reminiscences, but they've not been forthcoming and perhaps it's as well . . . I have gone back to work this term! Edward [Snell] was let down at the last minute and asked me if I'd take some top French. Not really my line – and I've not taught French for 20 years – but I thoroughly enjoy being at it again. He wants me to go on next term, but I've settled for doing the first half: there's just too much to do in the summer, especially in June and July . . . I hope to go to Lancing tomorrow for their match with Winchester. Tea with Thorold[1], Jagger[2], Shearwood[3] and Doggart[4] should be a stimulating affair.

The book was duly published in 1962, and was well received.

To faithful attenders (weather permitting) in the Parks or at Lord's, no figure has been more familiar than that of Mr Geoffrey Bolton, who can claim to have seen the whole or part of most Oxford-Cambridge cricket matches since 1913. He has employed the leisure of retirement in compiling, with egregious industry, a chronicle of Oxford cricket since its inception 135 years ago. The result is not only an encyclopaedic record, but a commentary enlivened by entertaining reflections and by many sidelights on the game and its development.

In his introductory 'Apologia', GB with his habitual modesty suggests that:

it should have been written by somebody with authority behind him, as it might be Sir Pelham Warner, one in a position to levy contributions from the great men of the past. I am in no such position, for I was never more than a member of my College side[5]; but my lot has been cast in pleasant places and I have watched a great deal of Oxford cricket. I cannot claim to approach the record of Dr Poynton, sometime Master of Univ., who told me in June 1939 that he had seen part of every match played in the Parks for 50 years; but I have seen part of *most* matches played there between 1913 and 1960. My chief justification for writing this book is my enthusiasm for Oxford cricket. Coming of a family exclusively Oxford on both sides, I have naturally developed a highly partisan attitude, but I have tried to keep it within bounds.

He goes on to deplore the decline in attendance at the varsity match and certain trends in cricket:

Nowadays a Cowdrey or a Sheppard is honoured, not for the making of a century in the Varsity Match, but for his feats against Australia. In the days when there were only eight first-class counties and no test matches, the fame of an Ottaway or a Yardley was made by what he did against Cambridge or Oxford. If those days are gone for ever, so be it. But to some of us old stagers, no matter whether we were good cricketers or bad, the Varsity Match is still *the* game of the year, as it must be to those who take part in it. May it never be ruined by the negative play of which we have seen (and read) so much in recent years . . .

A. J. Balfour once said that he could no longer go to the Eton and Harrow match – 'too many ghosts'; for the same reason, Francis Thompson would not go to Lord's, even to watch Lancashire. But surely the magic of the past can work another way. The old men back from Troy did not repine over the happy years 'before the war'; instead, they bored their wives and children into fits with their nightly spilling of salt and wine on the table as they made their sketch-maps illustrating their more-than-twice-told tales. I do not bore my neighbours at Lord's with my recollections of past Varsity Matches, but these recollections are very precious and one exults or shudders as they come to mind. The nearer I draw to the shadowy coast, the more determined I become to see as much as possible of each year's Varsity Match.

Summer Fields was by 1962 looking forward to, and planning for, its centenary in 1964. Among the many ideas to mark the occasion, an anthology of reminiscences was collected under the editorship of Richard Usborne, Old Summerfieldian, celebrated humorous writer in *Punch* and elsewhere, and the world authority on Wodehouse. There could have been no better choice, and he relied heavily upon GB, as he wrote in his 'Apologia':

> Only one person could write the proper history of Summer Fields – Geoffrey Bolton. He won't. He says there's not a book in it . . . The Governors, thwarted by GB's '*non potest*' or '*nolle prosequi*' (as his favourite Jeeves would say), passed a resolution, without asking me, that I should provide a book of some sort to mark the Centenary.

Later in the same introduction, he went on, 'I am grateful . . . to GB for being such good copy to so many generations of boys, and for correcting a lot of howlers at the proof stage.' He might also have added for producing so much copy; this book gave him the impetus to delve into his own memories, and articles on Fifth Form, the leagues and the Hitler war years resulted, several passages from which have been quoted earlier in this work. As for his *being* good copy, Usborne found that he had to slash articles dealing with the post-1918 era, for fear of *embarras de* GB.

> He read proofs for me, roaring (through the post) at howlers of fact, name and date, and correcting an ex-Regius Professor of Modern History who recalled that in 1902 he had been taken to see Victor Trumper make a century in the Parks. 'Strike out "The Parks", insert "Christ Church Ground".' GB had written a book about Oxford cricket, and anyway he was a walking *Wisden*. I didn't bother to check his correction with either the Professor or *Wisden*. I just accepted it.

In 1962, he also supplied an article for the school magazine on 'Summer Fields Bowlers, 1920–1962'. This was in celebration of an excellent cricket season, in ways even better than 1958, and a record-breaking bowling feat by Dennis Tabor. GB reminisced about Walter Savery in 1936–7, the Guinness brothers, Peter Carter and, more recently, Rupert Daniels and George Chamier.

Good as their figures are, they pale into insignificance beside those of Dennis Tabor. In 1960, he was a useful slow left-hander and took 17 wickets at 7.2. He then decided to bowl fast, and in 1961 he was a magnificent foil to Chamier, taking 49 wickets at 7.7. Between them, these two bowled over 400 overs in 16 matches, and very little change bowling was needed.

In 1962 Tabor was out on his own and all previous records were lowered. Although he missed one match, he took 82 wickets at an average of 3 . . . To any aspiring bowler who bothers to read this article I have but a word to add: Go thou and do likewise.

The winter of 1962/3 was extremely cold, and it got to GB.

Dudley Hotel, Hove. 11.2.63.

My dear Harold,

Thank you for yours, which finds me far from well & bored to tears. Such were conditions at Danny & from there to here that I told Edward I couldn't manage the teaching this term. But he was short already and nobly offered to put me up here. So I started term and in a week was down with bronchitis. I had over a week off duty, returned and lasted 3 days before the E. wind got at me again. I went back to bed y'day & am to stay there till after Wed. It isn't funny. I'm not bad this time, but am pretty lifeless and somehow – Heaven only knows how, for I can think of no possible cause – I have managed to wrench the shoulder of my bowling arm and can't even turn it over without great pain! My 1st answer to your question is

Quidquid delirant reges, plectuntur Achivi.

In other words, whatever loony subject Dick Usborne sets beaks to write on, they all turn to me for enlightenment. Roughly I can tell you a bit [Harold Hartley must have been asking questions about the school's buildings, the fruits of which would form his article in *A Century of Summer Fields*, 'Bricks and Stones', pages 43–53]:

Chapel was built as a memorial to "Mrs"; she died in '96, so presumably the date is '97.

New Room – some time in the early '90's.

Cubicles was the official school dining-room from I-don't-know-when till 1903. The dining-hall was built in 1903 & led to some litigation because it was built half on Maclaren & half on Williams land and the Maclarens weren't asked for permission. John & I suffered for this when we bought Cyril out; Pat or Perdie might be able to help here. But the cost. How <u>could</u> I know & where would I learn? What you mean by <u>etc</u> is not clear. I know nothing of the various additions to Mayfield. Cottage was run up in a great hurry c.1909: a typical Dogbags [i.e. Doctor Williams] building – no damp course & many of my books are ruined in consequence.

I had great trouble in getting the outside rears at F[ront] L[odge] de-ratted and rebuilt c.1926. "Rats?" said Dogbags, "that's nothing – put down some poison." But in the holidays he relented & had the job done. And that is all I can tell you of the buildings of S.F., Oxford.

Yours ever,
GB

At the school, preparations went ahead for the centenary celebrations. The first event of the Easter holidays was to be a dinner at Balliol College, with Harold Macmillan as the principal guest. From March and April 1964, there survive some letters from GB to Harold Hartley, which tell the sad story of his final weeks.

Danny, Hurstpierpoint, Sussex. 3.3.64.

My dear Harold,

As regards the dinner on April 3, of which I have as yet rec'd no notice, would it be convenient for Joan & you if I turned up on Thursday 2nd? My health hasn't been very good lately and I've got to take things quietly and avoid being rushed! Me, of all people! No doubt it's good for me spiritually, but I chafe.

I can see June 20 being very difficult in one way & another, but that fence needn't be crossed yet.

I am going, I hope, to stay with Mike S[haw] S[tewart] for the Calcutta Cup match. Edinburgh will be a great change from this, but won't be much colder than it is here today.

I think that Dick Us. has done a very good job in the S.F. book. I don't know how much you've seen of it, but Puss Henderson on Julian Amery is about the best of the whole lot.

Yours ever
GB

Will you tell Richard [presumably Porthouse] that I'll be sending him the balance of *Cricketers* after the Ides. I am delighted to find myself 2/6 up on him. I don't know when the return is.

* * * * *

Danny, Hurstpierpoint, Sussex. 26.3.64.

My dear Harold

I think our letters must have crossed. I have not yet given up the dinner for lost, as Edward will drive me to Newton and I think I'll (probably?) get up in evening dress!! What worries me now is, Can I cross the Balliol quad and negotiate any stairs there may be. 12 yards on 2 sticks is still my limit with grampus-like breathing at either end. *If* I can get over that, I've still got to exhibit myself to those who've always known me as Active to be completely Passive. Remains: to pray for a miracle – they do happen – and a supply of pluck. You shall be let know. Meanwhile, my hat is still in the ring.

Yours ever
GB

* * * * *

My dear Harold

An amendment. IF I get to the party (θεων ἐπι γούνασι κεῖται, or, as the Dr put it 5 mins ago, Pretty Dicey) Edward will be in charge, landing me at your door on <u>Friday</u> aft c.4.30 and bringing me back here at 10 next day. This at any rate is an enormous relief. I may even be dressed for the party when I arrive, to save breathing troubles, but that will depend on a lot of things.

I would put the odds at present at not worse [or more?] than 60–40 against. 12 yards on 2 sticks is my maximum walk at present and if we have to go upstairs at Balliol I shall be sunk. But I am so determined to be there that I feel possunt quia posse videntur will come to my help!

The only thing is I hope I shan't be a nuisance to you and Joan. Don't be alarmed at my desperate breathing: it subsides in 5 mins or so, and doesn't hurt.

Thanks for magazine, a good one but for the boys' 'poetry'. Did you see the death of F. E. Robeson, aet. 94, & engagement of Simon Hebeler, I forget who to (to whom)?

Well, ora pro nobis. Actually how <u>ill</u> I am I wouldn't know. I feel quite well except when on my feet but oh for sun, fresh air and a decent bath!

Yours ever

GB

A few days later, he suffered a thrombosis and was taken to hospital. He wrote from there to Pat Savage:

My dear Pat,

I have been carted off to Cuckfield Hospital, no private ward and a bloody row. I won't attempt to describe my feelings. Obviously I now have to scratch next week. I'll say as little as I can, but I don't think I've ever minded missing anything so much before. You will please give them all my love and say how sorry I am. I don't know if they're going to do anything for me here; if so I shall hope to be up for the Australians and on June 19 (Centenary Commemoration Day). Tell Harold, please. May you have the happiest of evenings.

Yours ever,

GB

Pat Savage read out GB's letter, expressing his misery and fury at the likelihood of his not being there, and, as Richard Usborne said in his obituary, to the last minute of that evening nobody was quite sure that GB *wouldn't* arrive, by hook or crook, ambulance or wheelchair, from Sussex.

For a lot of us, though, GB was there in spirit: gaunt, gauche, shy and a cause of shyness in others, challenging, abrupt, alarming; but a man of unforgettable stature and, though not himself a scholar, instiller of scholarship in others.

David James, MP for Brighton (Kemptown), was one of the many Old Summerfieldians who were at the dinner. Shortly after he had returned home, he went to see GB in hospital and report on the occasion.

Even to a layman it was evident that he was dying, but he wanted to know every detail, even though many brought tears to his eyes. When a nurse brought in his supper and told him to eat it up like a lamb, I thought how the mighty had fallen, until a familiar bellow told her to shut the – – – – – – – door.

Five minutes later I left, and five days later he died, but I shall always be grateful that chance enabled me to convey to him how much his absence had been felt.

GB's demise of course called forth various professional obituaries, but also inspired many of his former pupils to write in praise of what he had been to them and done for them. Let Denys Jameson (a Summer Fields pupil from 1931 to 1934) speak for these:

> To me he <u>was</u> the School, and I felt the greatest respect and, yes, affection, but terror too – I know just why the ancient Greeks kept out of the way of their gods. I look back on him as an Everest among molehills. I'm not at all sure that Charterhouse taught me <u>anything</u> I didn't already know from GB.

Hugh Stubbs, who was at Summer Fields from 1926 to 1930, muses on the possibility of GB's appearing in a work of fiction:

> Will GB's titanic personality baffle all description? There are plenty of fictional parallels for his sudden rages, real or assumed (I still remember the outburst of mixed English and Greek invective when I funked a rugger-tackle on Third Game), and his stern integrity is not uncommon ("He's the ONLY master who punishes you if you own up, and the ONLY master who won't let you off if you start to blub"). But never in fact or fiction have I come across so magnificent a teacher, one who touched nothing that he did not illumine, one whose forceful exuberance could leap in a moment over the gap between Cicero and Burke, Troy and Vimy Ridge, Euripides and P. G. Wodehouse. In class or out of it, he talked to us as a man of the world talking to men of the world.

Notes:

1. The Revd Henry Thorold, Old Summerfieldian, housemaster at Lancing, and later chaplain at Summer Fields before he retired to his country home, Marston Hall in Lincolnshire, where he continued to write excellent and expert books on ecclesiastical architecture and related topics.
2. Sam Jagger, a fine cricketer and squash-player, and author of a definitive book on squash. He was in charge of both at Lancing, as well as being a successful housemaster. He died quite suddenly aged only fifty-eight in the same year as GB.
3. Ken Shearwood, a gifted footballer and author of the history of Pegasus, the Oxford and Cambridge Old Blues' football club; a Salopian himself, he spent forty years at Lancing as a master and, later, registrar, retiring in 1996.
4. G. Hubert G. Doggart, of Cambridge, Sussex and England; cricket master and housemaster at Winchester. He wrote, inter alia, the biography of Harry Altham.
5. And he was probably only an occasional member at that, as the University College archivist can find no reference to him in the cricket teams of 1913–14.

CHAPTER 11: THE IMMORTAL PART

THERE WERE OBITUARIES in *The Times* by Richard Usborne and by Patrick Savage, and in *The Cricketer* by Eddie Harrison, secretary of the Sussex Martlets. Also a slip had to be prepared and inserted into *A Century of Summer Fields*, which said: 'Geoffrey Bolton, who stalks, very much alive, through the pages of this book, died yesterday. Too late for any *Vale* here, or alteration of present to past tenses.' Usborne amplified this brief remark in his obituary:

> The book will refer to a living GB throughout, as it was written. GB reading P. G. Wodehouse and W. W. Jacobs stories aloud in Cubicles and air-raid shelter; GB playing Gilbert and Sullivan on his gramophone; GB playing cricket (he wasn't very good himself, but the game was a sort of religion to him); GB roaring at Fifth Form for two and a half terms and cosseting them in their last weeks before scholarship exams; GB, when scholarships were over, won or lost, reading Homer with them, taking them to bathe in the river, taking them to the Parks, bowling to them in nets during prep; GB, no respecter of very important persons, either parents who may have been or boys who thought they were; GB driving his beloved car with a muttered monologue of execrations of pedestrians, bicyclists, road signs, road surfaces and all other motorists. GB's dislike of haddock, marmalade, cats and sloppy English.

PMBS, a few days later, added a perceptive Summerfieldian insight:

> In the small world of prep schools that he chose to work in, Geoffrey Bolton must surely rank as one of the very great teachers of this century. He confined himself to things that he could do really well and he put everything that he had got into them. He expected everyone else to do the same. He loathed anything second-rate or anything that smacked of shirking. His standards were exacting; his methods were expert; his speciality was preparing boys for public school scholarships – and especially Eton ones.
>
> His ideals and those of Summer Fields coincided exactly on most points. Though not a great classical scholar himself, he had a great veneration for the classics, and he was able to develop along his own lines the techniques bequeathed by his predecessors, themselves great men, when he took over the scholarship form. He inherited their knack of making boys find their work not tedious but exciting and challenging. But there was an element of terror in it all, and it was devotion and respect rather than affection that he inspired in his pupils, apart from a select few who managed somehow to get through his

defences. For on the surface there was a reserve amounting almost to austerity which made it hard for him to open his heart. So, when crises came, he had often to face them alone. Many grown-up people, especially boys' mothers, found him scaring. This was certainly not intended. He sought no pedestal. He was never patronizing or pompous, even to the smallest boy. It was a special kind of shyness.

It was to teaching and shaping boys' characters that he devoted himself with complete single-mindedness. (He rarely left the School in term-time – except to watch Oxford play cricket.) The routine administration of the School during his four years as Headmaster did not seem to give him the same satisfaction.

Though it is probably true that some mothers were afraid of him, it is equally true that others sent their sons to Summer Fields because of GB. He was not a misogynist, though he may well have thought that women had a 'place', and he would not have viewed feminism with much favour. But then people die at the right time: so much that the 1960s brought would have been anathema to him, and it is as well that he has been spared the changes in his beloved cricket which the forty years since his death have wrought. How he would have hated helmets, sledging, the oafish pseudo-excitement of the 'pyjama game' and the dreariness of modern test matches, with their tunelessly chanting football crowds! As Hubert Doggart said, what appealed to GB about cricket was its style, its serenity and its statistical interest. These still obtain in the game as played at prep schools, and perhaps some public schools and clubs; but only the last of the trio survives in most professional cricket.

GB lived to see the end of amateur status in cricket, and the final match was played between The Gentlemen and The Players in 1962. It witnessed a further apotheosis of David Sheppard, who, in the words of H. S. Altham, "returning to cricket after a break of some years, played an innings of 112 sound and resolute enough to ensure his place for Australia". That was to be his last tour abroad.

In 1965 the Sussex Martlets celebrated their diamond jubilee and produced a small follow-up to GB's 1955 booklet. It said that the chief architects of the club's growth over recent years had been Eddie Harrison and GB.

> Geoffrey Bolton, a great cricket enthusiast of the old school . . . devoted all his leisure hours to the Martlets and he set and expected a very high level of achievement and behaviour, both on and off the field. His insistence on maintaining the highest standards in all matters was of great value to the Club and he will be remembered as a great President . . . The death of the President in 1964 was an especially serious blow to the Club, but we are delighted that S. C. Griffith, the Secretary of MCC and a Martlet since 1938, has accepted the Presidency.

Wodehouse has gone from strength to strength, being held in high esteem by academics and general readers alike. There have been some very fair attempts at putting Jeeves and Bertie on television, and a rather less successful stab at Lord Emsworth, but nothing is as good as the books themselves, which read well on radio – often admirably adapted by Richard Usborne. There's a bit of a national schism about Gilbert and Sullivan at present; hordes of 'the faithful' continue to worship at the shrine, but others condemn these light and innocent operas as hopelessly *vieux jeu*, stuffy, sexist and generally politically incorrect. Jacobs and Buchan are mildly out of fashion, but possibly due for a revival in the hands of some enterprising director. The classics have had a tough battle, but receive occasional shots in the arm from Finnish radio stations and American educationalists. The market in marmalade and the popularity of cats as pets are booming; sloppy English rides triumphantly high, as do pomposity, journalese and officialese. So let us comfort ourselves with some limpid English, GB's obituary from the *Summer Fields Magazine* of 1964, by Bobs Alington.

I first met GB at Mayfield in, I suppose, the summer of 1919. I think he had come for an interview. As he was desperately shy, and my father almost inarticulate with strangers, I cannot believe that the interview went with a swing. I imagine that each recognized quality in the other instinctively, for they were devoted to one another ever after, though communication between them was confined to monosyllables, grunts and half-completed sentences.

At any rate, I was left to look after GB and half-way through the afternoon, after a lengthy silence, I asked him if he would care for a net.

'I should like nothing better,' he said. So out we went to the nets. I furnished him with bat, pads and gloves, and sent him in. After a while, I slowly began to realise how superbly bad he was as a cricketer.

I suppose he thought of little other than Summer Fields and Summerfieldians, cricket and cricketers, Gilbert and Sullivan operas and their casts, the Classics and classical authors, with occasional excursions into the worlds of French, P. G. Wodehouse and football. It was his delight to introduce generations of boys to these worlds of his. But, though he loved cricket and everything to do with it, he was a very indifferent performer; though he loved the Classics, he was not a real scholar; though he loved Gilbert and Sullivan, he was quite unmusical. And this was his glory. He had but two talents, and he went and gained other two.

I imagine that the greatest moment in GB's life was when he was invited to take on Fifth Form. Here was supreme confidence placed in him – nothing less than the future reputation of his beloved Summer Fields. We all know how he responded to this challenge . . .

To generations of Summerfieldians he was a figure of awe – tall, gaunt, white-haired, apparently arthritic, frequently turning his left wrist and arm over in the air, or playing imaginary strokes with an imaginary bat and a flat left elbow. His bark could be alarming, but was he really in a 'bate'? Eight times out of ten – no! He had grown up in a generation which was continuously shouted at, and shouting was *de rigueur* when he joined the Summer Fields staff. It was, to him, the natural way to keep order and promote industry. It meant little or nothing usually. But on the other two occasions he was probably exasperated, for he was a perfectionist. Failure on the part of those with whom he so thoroughly identified himself maddened him. It was like his own failure.

GB was essentially humble. He realised his limitations and accepted them, and made the best of what he had got, which was enough to turn him into a great schoolmaster – one who put the boys first, the school second, his teaching third, the rest of life fourth, and himself a bad fifth. Humility and experience had made him wise; his advice was always sound and usually cautious.

The last time I saw him was during his headmastership. He was standing at square-leg with a transistor, umpiring First Game and listening to a Test Match. I had to await his full attention till the end of two overs, one at Lord's and one at Summer Fields.

I like to think of him organising cricket in the Elysian Fields:

Odysseus, caught Aeneas, bowled Bolton, 0.

Touching upon the classics, we may perhaps end fittingly with a Latin tribute written for the school's centenary book by Mark Mortimer, GB's Eton 2nd scholar of the 1947 vintage:

> **G**rande opus est: dubito tantum celebrare magistru**M**
> **B**arbaricaque artem laedere laude tua**M**;
> **G**raecam a quo didici linguam didicique Latina**M**
> **B**rutus ad Aoniam te duce vectus aqua**M**.
> **G**ratia cui quae sit, conans ego dicere, fia**M**
> **B**laesus et os potero vix aperire meu**M**.
> **G**rata tamen brevitas: ne longo carmine vexe**M**,
> **B**is tantum hos versus quattuor obtuleri**M**.*

* It is a mighty task: I hesitate to sing the praises of so great a schoolmaster and to sully your art with my primitive tribute – you, from whom I learnt Greek and Latin, guided by you to the Aonian water (by Mount Helicon, the home of the Muses). When I try to express due gratitude, I become tongue-tied and can scarcely open my mouth. But there is pleasure in brevity; so as not to bore you with a long poem, I simply offer these eight lines. – To **GB** from **MM**.

BIBLIOGRAPHY

Amery, Julian: *Approach March: A Venture in Autobiography*, Hutchinson, 1973.

Austin, Jonathan: *The English Boys' Boarding Preparatory School 1918–1940*, PhD thesis, 1995.

Bird, Anthony & Hutton-Scott, Francis: *Lanchester Motor Cars*, Cassell, 1965.

Bolton, Geoffrey: *History of the O.U.C.C.*, Holywell Press, 1962.

Bolton, Geoffrey: *Recollections of Summer Fields*, unpublished, 1963.

Bolton, Geoffrey: *Sussex Martlets*, 1905–1955, privately printed, 1955.

Danziger, Danny: *Eton Voices*, Viking, 1988.

Gibbs, David: *Summers by the Sea,* the centenary history of the Sussex Martlet Club, 1905–2005, privately printed, 2005.

Green, Benny (ed.): *The Wisden Book of Cricketers' Lives*, Queen Anne Press, 1986.

Handford, Basil: *Lancing College*, Phillimore, 1986.

Heath, Graham: *One Hundred Years at the Sanctuary, 1855–1955*, privately published, 1955.

Lee, Christopher: *Tall, Dark and Gruesome*, W. H. Allen, 1977.

Martineau, G. D.: *A History of the Royal Sussex Regiment*, Moore & Tillyer, 1953.

Monro, F. R. D'O.: *Repton Cricket, 1901–1951*, George Over, 1953.

Payne, M., and Batchelor, L.: *Bygone Crowborough*, Phillimore, 1987.

The Reptonian, 1909–13.

The Repton School Register, 1957.

Stubbs, Hugh: *Headmasters and Others*, unpublished, c.1970.

Swanton, E. W. (ed.): *Barclays World of Cricket*, Collins, 1986.

The *Summer Fields Magazine*, 1897–2003.

Thomas, Bernard (ed.): *Repton, 1557 to 1957*, Batsford, 1957.

Usborne, Richard (ed.): *A Century of Summer Fields*, Methuen, 1964.

Vargas, Dale: *Belmont Hassocks,* the Rise and Demise of an English Prep School, privately printed, 2005.

INDEX

Abbott & Mansfield (Greek grammar) 27
Acheson, John, Earl of Gosford 135
Acland Nursing Home 64, 128
Aids to French Composition 83
Alamein 112
Albania 31
Alexander, Jonathan 127
Alington, A. F. (Bobs) 9, 37, 38, 39, 41–42, 64, 65, 67, 73, 77,81, 82, 90, 92, 93, 104
Alington, Adrian 37, 38
Alington, Revd E. H. (Uncle Hugh: the Bear) 9, 37, 40–41, 47, 52, 53, 56, 58, 61–62, 64, 65, 71, 75, 77, 87, 92, 93, 120
Alington, Geoffrey 37, 39, 41–42, 43, 45, 47, 68
Alington, Gillian (née Tanner, Mrs AFA) 65, 104, 137
Alington, Jack 37, 38, 40–41
Alington, Margaret (née Maclaren) 9, 37, 39, 40–41, 61, 65, 71, 75
Allen, G. O. 135
Altham, Harry S. 28, 29, 31, 32, 117 (note), 147 (note), 148, 150
Alton 42
Amery, Julian 73, 81, 88, 91, 135, 145
Anglice Reddenda 9, 78, 112
Angus 82
Anti-Authority League 89–90
Approach March 88, 151
Archbishop of Canterbury 21,
Aristotle 31
Armstrong-Macdonnell, John 118
Arundel 48
Ashdown Forest 22
Asiago 47
Asquith, Herbert 34
Asquith, Simon 133
Aubers Ridge 43
Austin, Jonathan 67
Australia 34
Authentics Cricket Club 32, 48, 54, 97

Baedeker raids 112
Balcon, Jonathan 82
Balfour, A. J. 143
Balliol College, Oxford 145, 146
Banbury Road 121, 124
Barber E. K. (Ken) 53, 54, 108–109
Barber, Kitty (née Williams) 37, 51, 108–109
Barclay, H. M. 74

Barclay, Tim 69, 99
Barclay's Book of Cricketers 101
Barrie, J. M. 108
Beacon Road, Crowborough 22
Beadon, Sister 14
Beer, Nicholas 139
Bell, Jimmy (JLB) 9, 62–63, 70, 81, 91, 116, 119, 120, 122, 125, 128, 131
Belmont School 27
Bemax 26
Bennett, Sterndale 53
Beresford, Lord Charles 33
Berkeley Mansions, Piccadilly 68
Berry, M. J. 99
Black Book 85, 128
Blackwell's Bookshop 122
Blatchford, Robert 32–33
Bloxham School 142
Blue Mantles 49
Body-line bowling 98
Boer War 39
'Bogi' 82
Bolton, Angela (sister) 26
Bolton, Chloe (mother) 21–22, 24, 25, 71
Bolton, Henry Lushington (father) 21, 71
Bolton, Joyce (sister) 20, 26
Bolton, Richard (Dick, brother) 26
Bolton, Thomas (GB's grandfather) 21
Bolton, Wilfred (brother) 20, 26, 68, 73
Bordon 39
Borthwick, Robin 113
Borva Notes 78,112,120
Borva, Summer Fields 120
Boswell, J. 68
Bouzincourt 45
Bowtell, Eric (EFB) 9, 16, 96–97, 121
Bradfield College 78, 82, 134
Branwell, R. M. 15
Brasenose College, Oxford 64, 92
Brighton 31, 112, 125
Bristol 129 (note)
Broke, Robin 82, 133
Broke, Simon 133
Brookfields, Lieutenant Colonel 39
Brook House, Repton 32
Broomstick Match 132–133
Browning Version, The 72–73
Buchan, John 151

Buckley, Hon. B. B. (Bryan) 15, 52, 53, 54, 60, 61
Burke 147
Burnett-Hitchcock, Basil 133
Burrows, Bernard 15
Butler, E. B. 15
Buxton, Sidney 33
Buzzer (Summer Fields shop) 107

Caesar, Julius 89
Calvert-Smith, David 132–133
Cambridge University 9, 16, 98, 112
Campbell, G. V. 48
Camperdown, Crowborough 22, 24
Canterbury Cricket Club, New Zealand 101
Cardus, Neville 31
Carlyon, Tommy 99–100
Carter, Peter 143
Case, Thomas 54
Case, W. S. (Billy) 52, 53, 57, 58, 59, 60, 61, 64, 65, 75, 87, 137
Century of Summer Fields, A 17, 137, 144, 149
Chalk, Gilbert 139
Chamier, George 139, 142–144
Charterhouse School 78, 81, 82
Chawton 42
Chaytors 38
Chips, Mr 71
Christ Church Ground 143
Cicero 147
Cinque Ports 37, 39, 42
Cinque Ports Gazette 45, 47
Claridge's Hotel 134
Classical Notebook, A 121
Clayton, Harold (HWC) 113, 124, 141
Clergy Mutual Assurance Society 21
Clifton College 82
Close, Bill 70
Close, Ted 70, 99
Cobham, Lord 135
Coghill, Nevill 74
Colman, Sir Jeremiah 49
Common Entrance 81, 100
Conan Doyle, Sir Arthur 48, 94
Corpus Christi College, Oxford 54
Corran, Andrew 123
Cothill House School 62, 74, 98
Cottage, Summer Fields 59, 65, 98, 104, 107, 108, 114, 115, 119, 121, 122, 125, 128, 144

County Houses Association 141
Coward, Noel 24
Cowdrey, M. C. 142
Cox, George 141
Cricket: Batsmanship 31
Cricketer, The 149
Crocker-Harris, Andrew 71, 73
Crofts, J. F. (Crab) 9, 40–41, 53, 54, 58, 59, 60, 61,137
Crowborough, 22, 24, 26
Cryptics Cricket Club 32, 50
Cubicles, Summer Fields 59, 60, 94, 104, 107, 114, 144, 149
Cuckfield Hospital 146
Cunningham, C. 63
Cunynghame I. F. R. 15

Daniels, Rupert 133, 143
Danny, Hurstpierpoint 24, 140–141, 144, 145, 146
Dardanelles 26, 68
Davies (one-term master) 64
Davies, Hugh 107
Davies, P. L. (Peter) 17, 127
De Arundel 48,
Derbyshire County Cricket Club 112
Dicky, D. O'R. 99
Dixon, E. J. H. (Budge) 107
Dobson, M. P. 108
Dobson, R. H. 99
Doggart, G. Hubert H. 142, 147 (note), 150
Donegan, Lonnie 138
Donne, L. V. 134
Donnelly, M. P. (Martin) 32, 101, 116, 121
Dover 42
D'Oyly Carte Opera Company 102, 108, 141
D'Oyly Carte, Rupert 102
Dragon School 112, 124
Drew, D. S. 82
Drones Club 68
Drums of the Fore and Aft, The 94
Dunkirk 112
Dunnett, Roderick 132
Dyer, Martin 139

Eady, Hon. Toby 127–128
Eastbourne College 82
Ednam, Viscount 91
Elysian Fields 152
Emsworth, Lord 148
Eton College 59, 78, 80, 81, 112, 114, 122, 125, 132, 133, 143, 149, 152

Eton Voices, anthology 92

Euripides 147

Evans, G. W. (Bam) 9, 15, 40–41, 52, 53, 54, 57, 64, 137

Evans, John (JFE) 9, 18, 45, 46, 52, 54, 58, 60, 61, 62, 65, 67, 68, 73, 77, 92, 93, 104 (and note), 105, 107, 108, 116, 117 (note), 118, 120, 123, 124 127, 128, 129, 131, 132

Exeter, Bishop of (*see Mortimer, Right Revd Robert*)

Exham, Percy G. 27–28

Eyre, Marjorie 102–103

Faber, Mark 134, 139

Faber, Michael 133, 134

Fanshawe, Major General 43

Fara 47

Farnborough School 105, 107, 110

Fawcus, M. E. 82

Fazan, Second Lieutenant R. 42

Feast at Midnight, A 104 (note)

Felsted School 82

Fifth Form 56, 58, 59, 62, 65, 77, 78, 80, 82, 95, 98, 100, 107, 110, 112, 120, 121, 123, 128, 143, 149, 151

Fifth Form B 82

Fisher, Francis 89

Fisher, Geoffrey 28

'Five Wise Men' 137

Flint, Russell 102

Ford, Lionel 28, 29

Ford, Neville 56

Foster, R. E. 117

Fox, James 113

Franz Ferdinand, Archduke 34, 35

Free Foresters Cricket Club 32, 125

Freeman, Godfrey 82

French Room 120

Freyberg, General Paul 122, 135

Frodsham, Geoffrey (GSF) 67

Front Lodge, Summer Fields 54, 55, 59, 104, 107, 114, 116, 144

Fry, Charles Burgess 30, 31, 48, 116–117, 129

Gables, The, Crowborough 22–23

Gardner, school butler 121

Gilbert and Sullivan 16, 24, 27, 37, 102, 108, 139, 141, 149, 150, 151

Gilbert, W. S. (*see Gilbert and Sullivan*) 16, 24, 27, 147, 148, 149

Gilligan, A. E. R. 50

Girl on the Boat, The 94

Gladstone, W. E. 54

Gmelin, Mrs 40–41

Gmelin, Revd C. H. S. 40–41, 85, 114
Goldsmith Avenue, Crowborough 22
'Golgotha' 19
Gonnehem 43
Gordon, Chloe (*see Bolton, Chloe*) 21
Gorsedene, Crowborough 22
Gosford, Earl of (*see Acheson, John*)
Gover, Mike (Guv) 124
Grange, The, Crowborough 27
Granville, Sydney 102
Greek Grammar, A 83
Greek Vocabulary, A 83
Gregory, S. E. 102
Grewal, Robin 139
Greycotes School 137
Griffith, S. C. 150
Griffiths, W. H. 116
Guinness brothers 143
Guinness, Edward 82
Gunn, John 102

Hall, The, Repton 34
Hamble, River 31
Hampshire County Cricket Club 32
Hampshire Hogs 32
Hardy, Nina 24–25
Harlequins Cricket Club 32
Harris, Lord 21
Harrison, Eddie 134, 149. 150
Harrow School 78, 82, 143
Hartley, C. E. 63
Hartley, Harold (HWLH) 9, 63, 91, 121, 144–146
Hartley, Joan 145,146
Hartshorne, Frank 63, 70
Haskoll, Mrs 40–41
Haskoll, T. J. F. 40–41
Hassocks 27
Haw-Haw, Lord 22
Hayward, Tom 62, 137
Hebeler, Simon 146
Henderson, Derek 112–113, 124, 125
Henderson, Sir J. Nicholas (Nico) 9, 62–63, 145
Henry V 74
Herodotus 75
Hext, J. W. 70, 99
Hill, Clem 116–117
Hill, Lowry 137

Hill, the Misses, Rhoda and Mildred 137
Hirst, George 102
History of the O.U.C.C. 32, 34, 73, 1152, 141–143
Hobbs, J. B. 102
Holmes, Sherlock 68
Homer 13, 29, 80, 110, 149
Hope, Anthony 37, 94
Hornung, E. W. 37
Horris Hill 37, 85, 98, 134
Hossell, Charles H. 112–113, 123, 124, 125
House, Summer Fields 107
Hove 48, 71, 123, 141
Hulbert, Ralph 127
Human Boy, The 94
Hunter, P. G. 74
Hurstpierpoint 140–141, 145, 146
Hyde White, Wilfred 13

Iliad 14, 122
Iolanthe 69, 141
I Zingari Cricket Club 32, 54

Jackson, Mike 68
Jacobs, W. W. 94, 112, 137, 149, 151
Jacques, Roger (RAKJ) 67, 88, 92, 93, 104
Jacques, Ruth 93
Jagger, Sam 142, 147 (note)
James, David 82, 98, 99, 146
James, M. R. 95
Jameson, Denys 147
Jeeves 68, 137, 143, 150
Jeeves and the Old School Chum 94
Jeffreys-Jones, Llewellyn 67
Jenkins, Herbert 73
Jerram, C. S 78
Jessop, Gilbert 102
Johnson, Samuel 68
Johnston, Brian 95
Jones, Micky 125
Jungle Book, The 94
Junior Latin Composition 83
Junior Martlets 125

Kaleidoscope 26
Kaplowitch, Nicholas 133
Kay, David 63, 91
Kay, Peter 132

Keble College, Oxford 92, 102
Keep, Hugh 133
Kendall, Henry 124
Kennedy (Latin grammar) 27, 83
Kidd-May, David 116
Kidd-May, Joanna 116
Kidd-May, Sarah-Jane 116
King's Royal Rifle Corps 32
King's Standing Station 22
Kipling, Rudyard 37, 68, 73, 94

Lanchester cars 112, 114, 119
Lanchester, Frederick 21
Lancing College 48, 142, 147 (notes)
Langham, Lieutenant Colonel, F. G. 39
'Lawson-Clauson gang' 98
Leave It to Psmith 94
Lee Bolton & Lee 21
Lee, C. F. C. (Christopher) 17, 70, 96, 104 (note)
Lee, Henry Wilmot 21
Lee, John Benjamin 21
Le Havre 43
Lehmann, John 87
Letts, Anthony 133
Lewis, Bertha 102
Leyland, Maurice 116
Library, Summer Fields 107
Liddell & Scott (Greek Lexicon) 75
Life's Handicap 94
Lillers 43
Lister, Guy 100
Literae Humaniores (Greats) 34
Little Nugget, The 94
Lloyd George, David 91, 96
Lody, Carl Hans 43
Lomax, Derek 85
Long Chamber, Eton 59, 80
Loos 45
Lord's 142, 152
Love among the Chickens 94
Lovett, Nancy 128, 137
Lower Fifth 82
Lower Remove 78
Lowndes, Peter 139
Ludgrove School 127
Ludlow 112
Lynam, Joc 124

Lysaght, Revd J. A. C. (Liz) 9, 52, 53, 100, 108, 120
Lytton, Henry 71, 102, 141

Mackay, Hon. J. L. 99
Maclaren, Archibald 9, 37, 40–41, 57, 142,
Maclaren, Cecil 40–41
Maclaren, Ethel 40–41
Maclaren, Gertrude 9, 37, 53, 57, 93, 104, 144
Maclaren, Wallace 37, 40–41
Macmillan, Lady Dorothy 135
Macmillan, Harold 131, 134–136, 145
Macnee, Patrick (Smee) 9, 63, 70, 73, 74
Macpherson, R 133
Magdalen College School 48, 73
Malvern College 82
Manor, Summer Fields 59
Mansel-Carey, David 108
Marlborough College 37, 82
Marsden, H. K. (Bloody Bill) 79–80
Marston Ferry Road 121
Marston Hall, Lincolnshire 147 (note)
Marston, Nichol 135
Marston, Pat (JPM: the Ogre) 9, 102, 116, 125, 131, 142
Marston, Perdita (née Williams) 9, 137, 142
Martineau, Susan 11
Martlets, Sussex 14, 32, 48, 50, 102, 108, 124, 125, 126, 134, 149, 150, 153
Marylebone Cricket Club (MCC) 32
Mayfield, Summer Fields 37, 45, 59, 65, 104, 108, 144, 149, 157
McKenna, David 15
Mens Sana in Corpore Sano 57
Mercury, training ship 31
Middle Fourth 121
Middlesex County Cricket Club 101
Middleton, B. H. 91
Middleton, Colin 139
Mikado, The 141
Mike 32, 68
Mike and Psmith 32, 94
Miles, T. R. (Tim) 17, 63
Milne, A. A. 37, 94
Modernside 82
Money for Nothing 94
Moor Park School 112
Mordaunt, David J. 125, 126, 134
Morgan, Miss 115, 119–122
Morning Post 61
Mortimer, Edward 129 (note)

Mortimer, Mark 125, 129 (note), 152
Mortimer, Right Revd Robert, Bishop of Exeter 125, 134
Mowden School 126, 141
Mullins, Hubert (HMM) 67, 82

Neuve Chapelle 43
New Room, Summer Fields 97, 135, 137
New Theatre, Oxford 122
New Zealand 101, 116
Newcombe, S. L. 91
Newton, Summer Fields 145
Nijinsky 100
Normandy Landings 112
Norrie, General Willoughby 135
North Oxford Cricket Club 97

O'Byrne, W. 125
Odyssey 14, 122
Old Lodge, Summer Fields 59
Oldham, Derek 102
Orchard, The, Repton 27, 30
O'Rorke, D. E. 15
Oxford University Cricket Club 14, 48, 125

Paget, N. D. 82
Paget-Cooke, R. A. 91
Pancras, SS 43
Parks, The 62, 71, 101–102, 115, 122, 124, 137, 142, 143
Parsons, Rupert 139
Passchendale 91
Patcham 39
Pegasus Football Club 147 (note)
Peirce, Miss Lilwall, (Cussus) 59–60, 87
Penny, Frederick P. 9, 52, 53, 54, 59, 60–61, 67, 87, 137, 158
Peter Pan 108
Pioneers 45
Pitt, William 39
Plato 32
Playhouse, Oxford 122
Point, Jack 71
'Polyglotshire' 16
Poole, Christopher 82, 132–133
Poole, J. J. 70
Pope, Lieutenant R. M. 42
Porchester Terrace 22
Porter, Russell 69
Porthouse, Richard (RNP) 136, 143

Poynton, J. B. 142
Prichard, Francis 125
Priestley, N. deB. 15
Prince, Dr Leeson 22
Prince of Wales (later Edward VIII) 39
Pryor, Revd W. L. A. 118
Psmith 68
Punch 34–35, 94, 143
Purchas, Bob 63
Pusey House 119, 121

Queen Anne's Bounty 21

Radley College 82, 125, 127
Rae, Alison, 11
Raffles 49, 68, 73
Rands, Leslie 102–103
Ranjitsinhji, K. S. 48, 49, 65
Rattigan, Terence 72
Rawstorne, L. A. 118
Recollections of Summer Fields (by GB) 11, 26
Rendel, Guy 26
Rendel, Herbert and Reginald 26
Repton School 27, 29, 30, 56, 82, 85
Reptonian, The 29, 32
Rhys-Williams, G. D. 63
Richard II 74–75
Ridge, Vimy 147
Right Ho, Jeeves 94
Roberts, David 139
Roberts, Jonathan 134
Roberts, Lord 33
Roberts, R. A. 63
Robeson, F. E. 146
Robinson, Ralph (RWGR: Rhino) 52, 67, 108
Rodgers, Piers 133
'Roots and Tweaks' 96
Rouen 43
Royal Sussex Regimentt 34, 35, 39
Royle 102

Sadler's Wells 141
Sanctuary, The 21, 23
Sandbach, R. M. 15
Sapper 94
Sarajevo 37
Saunders, Christopher J. 125, 126

Savage, Patrick (PMBS) 9, 11, 107, 114, 116, 119, 120, 122, 125, 128, 129, 131, 134, 137, 138, 146, 149
Savery, Walter 99, 143
Seager, Gerald 98–100
Secrets of a Savoyard, The 102
Sedbergh School 82
Serbia 34
Shaw, George Bernard 13, 73
Shaw, Henry (Captain) 63, 69
Shaw-Stewart, Michael 69, 145
Shaw-Stewart, Patrick 63, 69, 70
Shearwood, Ken 142, 147 (note)
Sheffield, Leo 102
Sheppard, David S. 127, 142, 150
Sherborne School 142
Ship Hotel, Brighton 125
Shrewsbury School 82
Sikes, H. L. S. 15
Sinclair, Robin 73, 74
Slade, Christopher 105, 110
Slade, Julian 108, 110, 111
Smith, Richard 133
Smyth, C. E. 52, 53, 54, 56, 58, 61, 64, 85, 137
Snell, Christopher 125, 126, 141
Snell, Edward 125, 141, 142, 145, 146
Somervell, D. C. 32, 33, 34
Somerville College, Oxford 45
Something Fresh 94
Somme, The 45
St Cyprian's, Eastbourne 108
St Edward's School 9, 82, 112, 123, 124
St John's College, Cambridge 27
Stalky & Co. 68
Standring, Denis 108
Starkey, Simon 125
Stephenson, E. K. (Tubby) 107
Stevenson, R. L. 94
Stewart, D. L. L. 63
Stowe School 82
Strachey, Lytton 13
Strand Magazine 94
Straton-Ferrier, Brian 24, 82, 98–100, 104 (note), 117 (note)
Straton-Ferrier, John 24
Stratton's, Repton 34
Strong, Leonard A. G. 15, 50 (note), 52, 53, 54, 57, 60–61, 81, 88, 137
Stubbs, Hugh 94, 147
Sturt, Guy 12

Sullivan, Arthur (*see Gilbert and Sullivan*)
Sullivan Cigarettes 73
Summer Fields 5, 9, 11, 13, 14, 16, 17, 18, 26, 37, 38, 39, 45, 47, 48, 50, 51, 53,
   56, 58, 59, 60, 62, 63, 64, 67, 70, 71, 74, 75, 77, 80, 81, 82, 85, 88, 89, 93, 96,
   97, 98, 104, 107, 108, 110, 112, 113, 116, 121, 123, 125, 126, 127, 129, 131,
   134, 137, 139, 141, 143, 147 (note), 149, 150, 151, 152
Summer Fields Herald, The 86–87
Summer Fields Magazine, The 83, 87, 106, 151, 153
Summer Fields St Leonard's 38, 39, 108, 116
Summer Lightning 94
Surtees, Repton 34
Sussex County Cricket Club 110, 123
Sussex Martlets, (*see Martlets*)
Sutcliffe, Herbert 134
Swanton, E. W. (Jim) 121

Tabor, Dennis 139, 143–144
Tabor, Robert 133
Tamworth, Ian 15, 85
Tanner, Gillian (later Mrs AFA) 65
Temple, William 28, 29, 32
Thesiger, Ernest 13
Thicknesse, R. 63
Thomas, Asa 48
Thomas, gents' hairdresser 17
Thompson, A. A. 133
Thompson, Francis 143
Thompson, R. Stanley 142
Thomson, A. W. H. (Stodgy) 9, 108
Thorold, Revd Henry 142, 147 (note)
Thucydides 75
Times, The 95, 149
Tomlinson, Bill 108–109, 112
Tomlinson, Bud 108–109
Tonbridge School 82
Tower of London 42–43
Trapnell, B. M. V. 116
Trevaskis, (Sir) Kennedy 74
Trinity College, Oxford 123, 125
Troy 147
Trumper, Victor 143

Ukridge 68
United Services 50
Universal, The (magazine) 86
University College, Oxford 36, 92, 147 (note)
Upper Remove 78

Uppingham School 29
Usborne, Richard A. (Dick) 17, 104 (note), 143–145, 146, 150

Varsity and Public Schools Camp 127
Vergil 85
Vice Versa 94
Vinery/Vins 60

Wadham College, Oxford 31
Wandering Minstrel, A 102
War, Great (WW1) 13, 14, 34
War, Second World (WW2) 22
Warner, Sir Pelham 142
Warwickshire County Cricket Club 101
Watson, Dr J. 68
Wee Willie Winkie 94
Wellington College 82, 101
Wellington Cricket Club 101
Wells, H. G. 13, 73
Wembley 141
Westminster Abbey 21
Westminster School 82, 108
White, Richard 113
Williams, Charles E. E. (the Doctor) 26, 37, 39, 40–41, 47, 50, 53, 57, 58, 59, 65, 77, 82, 83, 92, 93, 104, 108, 109, 120, 144
Williams, Cyril (CAEW) 40–42, 53, 54, 57, 58, 64, 77, 78, 80, 83, 85, 90, 92, 93, 98, 104, 144
Williams, Duncan 134, 138
Williams, Hermione (née a'Beckett Terrell) 53
Williams, Hilary 37, 39, 40–41, 45
Williams, Kitty 40–41
Williams, Mabel (née Maclaren) 37, 40–41, 47, 50
Wilson, David 82, 133
Winchester College 82
Windsor Castle 122
Winn, Chris 125
Wisden (cricketer's almanack) 27, 143
Wodehouse, P. G. 9, 16, 37, 73, 94, 95, 108, 112, 137, 143, 147, 149, 150, 151
Womersley, Mike 112–113, 125
Wood, George 48
Woodcote House 78
Woolley, Frank 116
Wooster, Bertie 68, 150
Worcester College, Oxford 117 (note)

Yeomen of the Guard, The 71
Ypres, Battle of 43, 45, 47

16·2·

my dear Stanley

thankyou so much for your letter and for
promising to get a copy of the bo
hope it will come out in April: I
xford recently and they seemed hopef
Jes, I wondered what you would think
in Swanton's effort!
ind & helpful that
him. The book h
do. I could have
originally I had
reminiscences, but
perhaps it's as
delighted to hear th
, F. next term. Also
hurt. I will make a point of bring

Brian Sk

The

Ha